WHEN FURY TAKES OVER

JOHN FURY

WHEN FURY TAKES OVER

MY BARE-KNUCKLE LIFE AS HEAD OF THE FURY FAMILY

WITH RICHARD WATERS

MACMILLAN

First published 2023 by Macmillan
an imprint of Pan Macmillan
The Smithson, 6 Briset Street, London EC1M 5NR
EU representative: Macmillan Publishers Ireland Ltd, 1st Floor,
The Liffey Trust Centre, 117–126 Sheriff Street Upper,
Dublin 1, D01 YC43
Associated companies throughout the world
www.panmacmillan.com

ISBN 978-1-0350-1405-7 HB
ISBN 978-1-0350-1406-4 TPB

Copyright © John Fury 2023

3 5 7 9 8 6 4 2

A CIP catalogue record for this book is available from the British Library.

Typeset in Fairfield LT Std by
Palimpsest Book Production Ltd, Falkirk, Stirlingshire

Printed and bound by CPI Group (UK) Ltd, Croydon, CR0 4YY

Visit **www.panmacmillan.com** to read more about all our books
and to buy them. You will also find features, author interviews and
news of any author events, and you can sign up for e-newsletters
so that you're always first to hear about our new releases.

For my son Tyson, without whose remarkable achievements in boxing there would be no book or such interest in the Fury family.

'No one can ever say they
beat John Fury on the cobbles.'

Contents

He's still a fighter, and I believe that
fire will never go out until he takes
his last breath – Tyson Fury

Foreword

My dad is truly a man among men. He's made a man of all his six boys – they all stand on their own two feet and rely on nobody but themselves. In life you only have your family, family is everything to us, and John Fury is our clan leader. Things were hard for him growing up and he had to fight his way through life. He never wanted that for us boys, thanks to him and my mum we had a privileged upbringing.

It's my hope that this book will reveal some of the lesser-known sides of my dad, and not just the obvious ones. Yes, he's still a fighter, and I believe that fire will never go out until he takes his last breath, but my dad also loves walking, history, old films and travel. Most importantly, my father is a man of God, he read the good book constantly while he was in prison and lives by it in deed. As you'll learn, he is a person who loves nothing more than to help others, and this is the real John Fury.

Tyson Fury, 2023

She looked at my bloody shirt
and said, 'Go back and fight him
until you know you've won.'

1

On the Road

I was born in 1965 on the side of a road in a bow-top Gypsy wagon, in a place called Tuam in the beautiful hills of County Galway, Ireland. I was lucky enough to spend the first three years of my life on the Emerald Isle, and part of me is still there. Whenever life takes me to Ireland I feel most at home, and though I like the people very much, for they are my people, it is the land that speaks to me, that runs through my veins to my heart. It's my heritage; here the ghosts of my ancestors sit around peat fires singing and telling stories by the glow of the flames. In those days you could go anywhere you felt like, with complete freedom to roam and set up camp, and when the Fury family stopped for a few days, they always cleaned up after themselves and left the area immaculate – no one would have known we'd ever been there.

I come from a poor background. We had two vehicles: one a van, the other a trailer (non-Traveller folk would call it a caravan). And while I say we were poor in one way, we were rich in another, as there was an abundance of love in my family. To us children, my parents were affectionate and kind but strict as hell.

My parents met at the Doncaster horse races, on St Leger Day in September, 1960. They say opposites attract – well, just as my parents were chalk and cheese, so too were their families. My father's side of the family – the Furys – sold linoleum, soft furnishings, carpets and rugs from door to door. It was called 'hawking'. They were smart people who possessed great people skills. This was down to the fact that they might knock on 500 doors in a single day, having conversations with so many different types of people and absorbing knowledge. On my mother's side, the Skeets were hard-working manual labourers, who possessed a gameness and energy about them. Both families were proud and immaculately tidy and brought their kids up strictly.

Though I may hail from a long line of boxers and fighters, my father was non-confrontational and never entered the ring himself. At the first sign of raised voices or arguments, he would remove himself from the vicinity, not because he was a coward he just hated conflict. You may wonder where my gladiatorial streak comes from. The answer is my mother. She had a dangerously fiery temper, and that is putting it mildly!

My earliest memory is seeing my father climb on top of a tin-roofed barn to get some pigeons. I was only three years old and, as we watched him fall through the roof, I thought I'd lost my dad for ever. My mum came out of the trailer, also thinking he was dead, and then to our relief we heard him wailing, 'I've broken my back! I'm going to spend the rest of my life in a wheelchair!' But as we inched closer to the barn with trepidation, my mother at the head of us, on closer inspection we saw he was absolutely fine. 'There's not a broken bone in your body, Hughie,' said my mum, 'You landed on a bloody hayrick!'

Being an Irishman, whether it was fair to say he had the 'luck of the Irish' remains up for question; after all, he had me for a son, and I was nothing if not a headache. I'll admit I was a bit of a scrapper from the start. The first ever fisticuffs I can remember happened when I was just five years old. We'd left Ireland by then and were wintering in Derbyshire. That sounds rather grand. What I mean is that my family had pulled up at a holiday campsite for a few days because our truck was in need of repair. It was snowing, and there was a fair bit of it sticking on the ground. I saw what looked like a nine-year-old, who looked mean as a farmyard cat, picking on a small lad, pushing him around a bit. I don't know why I didn't scare of him, probably because the little lad he was bothering was my own kin, my younger brother Peter, and he was only three years old at the time. I have always had a problem with bullies picking on those who are weaker than them, just as I've always been compelled to back the underdog.

Anyway, I'm straight over to them, placing a gentle hand on Peter's shoulder and separating the two. Then I square up to the tomcat, and it's as if my hands naturally know to ball themselves into two fists, with the thumbs always on the outside so they don't break when you hit something. They now look like medieval maces covered in skin at the end of each arm. The first mace connects with the bully's cheekbone, and he looks at me wide-eyed, clearly not used to being hit this hard by a five-year-old.

So, we fight on for a few minutes in the falling snow, steam shooting out of our noses like bullocks silently going at it. And next thing we are tussling on the frozen ground of the campsite, rolling ourselves into a hidden nest of barbed wire. I can feel the spikes going into my belly, arms and legs, but one thing they should have told the lad about the Furys is we protect our own and we never give up. Ever. Doesn't matter how many times we get punctured, kicked, or punched, we never quit.

Spattered in each other's snot and blood, the older boy waves his hand in submission and says, 'That's enough of this!' The red mist clears from my head and I've saved my little brother from this bully, that's all I care about. I say to my adversary, 'Are you finished?' He nods and that's that. I'm worried that my jumper is ripped and covered in blood, and what my mother is going to say about that.

But when she sees me a moment later as I'm getting ready to take a good hiding, she simply says, 'Well, did you win?'

'I don't know,' I said, 'I think I might have.'

She looked at my bloody shirt and said, 'Go back and fight him until you know you've won.'

The kid's mother got involved then and started insulting my mother. 'Stay away from us, you itinerant Gypsies.' And with that my mum hit her twice. Fortunately, my dad – ever the peacekeeper – arrived just in time to grab my mum and usher her away to the trailer, but the owner of the site said we had to leave that day.

There were four of us boys, and we were all born within a year of each other. My older brother was called Hughie. After Hughie I came along, then there was Jimmy the third boy, and finally our youngest brother, Peter. Brother Hughie may as well have been a reincarnation of my mother and grandfather, so alike was he to them in character; he was completely fearless, lawless, and intrepid. Where I would brood over the consequence of something, he would swat away my worries as if they were flies and, with that special charisma he possessed, convince me to follow him. Like the time we nabbed a couple of chickens and started to breed them a few fields away from the caravan site. I was his wingman – what he did, I did.

Jimmy was the odd one out among us wild ruffians. Much like my dad, he avoided all conflict and was a highly social person who went to the pub every day as he didn't like being on his own. He was also a true Traveller, and lived in a caravan till the end of his days.

And finally, there was Peter. Of all the brothers Peter was, and still is, the smart one. He's been around boxing all his life and, even though as a fighter he only had one amateur fight, what he doesn't know about boxing isn't worth knowing.

Wherever one Fury brother went, the others followed; we came as a kind of clan. And if you were daft enough to challenge one, you had the rest of us to deal with. While three out of four brothers had that dangerously incendiary spark, which was as easily flicked on as a light switch, it was tempered by the intelligence of our father's genes. We'd been raised not to look for trouble. My dad used to say, 'If somebody is nice to you, be nice back to them.' Secretly, we hoped that somebody wouldn't be nice to us, which would give us an excuse to fight. The moment somebody tried to be clever and take the mickey out of us, that was that, the gloves were off. The Fury brothers took no prisoners; you'd get a crack in the lug, a punch in the earhole, and we only asked questions afterwards.

Curiously, as a family, we didn't spend that much time with other Travelling folk, as my dad was suspicious of pretty much everyone. As such, we were independent and did things our way, avoiding waste ground to pitch up beside other Gypsies. Instead, we parked in fields, council-run campsites, pub car parks or farms. My dad used to say that if we went to a Gypsy camp there would always be one puffed-up fool who thought he was the King of the Gypsies, and before long he would be trying to incite my dad to violence. But my dad was a quiet man and didn't like confrontation. He would always say to his boys, 'No fighting, just keep your noses clean and stay away from trouble.' But did we listen? Course we didn't!

In spite of my dad's wise words, my parents fought each other like cat and dog. Mum was made of hard stuff and in the past she'd done manual labour, Tarmacking, barn painting, you name it. She was a natural southpaw and could fight like a man using both her fists. Seeing my parents go at it hammer and tongs in the trailer was far from an infrequent event. I think my mother had one of the worst tempers that I've ever seen on a woman. My father you could do business with, you could talk him around, but not my mother. If you got on the wrong side of her, you were getting it, and there was no two ways about it.

The only people who really inspired me growing up were my mum and dad. Dad could see around corners, he always knew what was coming; it was as if he could see a problem happening before it occurred. He was a great student of human nature; he watched people closely and understood them. I'm not far off fifty-eight years old as I write this, and looking back over a life in which I've met many people, from famous actors to celebrated fighters (even The Greatest, Muhammad Ali, albeit very briefly as he signed a copy of his book for me), but I can honestly say my father was one of the most naturally intelligent individuals

I've ever known. It didn't matter that he could neither read nor write, he had a great mind in him. He got these smarts from his mum, my gran, who was another person with a great deal of naturally endowed wisdom. She'd say, 'Slow down, son, give things plenty of thought before you act. Anything done in a rush is no good. If you rush a bowl of soup it won't work.' There are other things that she said which will always stick in my mind: 'Anything done in a rush nine times out of ten is wrath' and, 'Be a good judge of character with the people around you.'

I'm afraid I didn't take much heed of the wisdom on the perils of rushing and wrath, though. Not a week went by in my childhood when I wasn't fighting. There was a lot of racism against Travellers back then, and little John Fury spent his childhood evening up the odds.

'Gypsy, Gypsy lives in a tent, can't afford to pay the rent.' If somebody threw me a jibe like that I just looked at them and said, 'Right, that's it, we're fighting. Come on, let's have you.'

I didn't care how many of them there were, nine times out of ten there would be three boys I'd have to contend with. There aren't many Furys who won't fight. I used to watch my dad take a lot of stick and he would always talk things down and defuse the situation. I used to think, 'That's unfair, there's no need for one man to put another down and treat him like that because he lives in a trailer. When somebody insulted my dad, I felt that red rage grow inside me: *Dad, you should hit him!* I'd think.

By the time I was fifteen or sixteen, nobody could put the brakes on me, not even my dad who I loved and respected. I'd become a force of nature. If anybody cheeked my father, I'd let them have it. As time went on, people came to know what I was like and it happened less often because they knew I would blow a gasket.

On my dad's side there was a mixture of keen intelligence and paranoia. He was very questioning about certain people, and more often than not his judgement proved right. Travellers live by their wits – they have to, that's all they've got, as most have had very little education. If you think about it, Gypsies have roamed the face of this planet for thousands and thousands of years, and despite persecution and constant suspicion, not to mention an attempted genocide in the Nazi death camps, they are still here. That's what I call resilience.

Traditions and knowledge have been passed down orally from generation to generation. I've got two hundred years' worth of Gypsy lore in this skull of mine. Our kind have always had to be social chameleons; we had to learn to mimic the ways, mannerisms and speech of house dwellers (ordinary folk), because if somebody knew you were a Gypsy, they'd have nothing to do with you, nor your wares, and you'd starve to death. So, we learnt from the moment we were little how to speak properly, taking our time to pronounce words clearly so that we spoke even better English than the house dwellers. The people whose doors we knocked on to sell our goods to, we treated with the upmost respect, as they were the ones who were ultimately feeding us, they were our living. When we went out to work, from nine a.m. till four p.m., we were living a lie. If I was to knock on someone's door and say, 'Good morning, madam, my name is John and I'm from the Gypsy encampment just down the road. Now, can I interest you—' I wouldn't have made it to the end of the sentence, the door would've been slammed in my face, and I would've been branded a vagabond: 'Get off my land!'

So we learnt to put our best foot forward. I was big for my age, when I was nine years old I was doing the work of a fourteen-year-old: Tarmacking, roadwork, painting and decorating. Tarmacking was real work. I loved the smell of the Tarmac, especially when you took the sheet off it. We used to buy it from the quarry, and then my dad would keep a sheet over it to keep it moist and soft. Its smell was magical, a bewitching aroma of petrol and tar mixed together. Sounds mad, but I used to put my finger in it or lick it as if it was liquorice. It was always stuck to my clothes and my hair as well, but I loved it.

For sales work I used to be well dressed, I'd have a tie and smart blazer on, my shoes polished, my hair washed, combed and side-parted, my teeth brushed. I was learning to be somebody else from a young age. People found me oddly precocious. There I was, a door-to-door salesman, a boy doing a man's job. And because of the quirkiness of it, they felt compelled to listen to this somewhat articulate boy.

I have very few memories of being a kid and doing nothing. Most of the time I was working, grafting from an early age, but these were golden days nevertheless. In the summer we'd get up at six thirty in the morning and finish work at ten o'clock at night. We worked flat-out, painting barns, Tarmacking, and whitewashing houses. We used to call the latter 'snowcemming', after 'SNOWCEM', the whitewash product. For all the time that there was daylight there was money to be made, and so we were working. One thing I am grateful for is that my mother insisted that myself and my brothers went to school, at least during the winter.

I think one of my favourite childhood places was Yorkshire. In the mid-1970s, when I was ten years old, all the pits were still open, and the colliers earned quite a bit more than the average person. They had cash to spend and weren't afraid to spend it and, come the weekend, they let their hair down. But no matter how many drinks they put away on a Saturday night, they were always on time for work. Miners were decent, proud people; they'd get up before dawn, before it was light, and disappear into the mouth of a pit, only to rise from the grimy depths, their faces blackened with soot. It took some bottle to go down into the bowels of the earth, working in the claustrophobic darkness. Colliers lived in tight communities and, though they were rough and tough folk, there was no edge to them; perhaps any sharpness got rounded off in the darkness. When you knocked on their door, they treated you as they treated everybody, with respect and an interest in what you had to say. Nine times out of ten you could sell to them; it was easy work, and Mum and Dad loved them.

I remember the summer of 1969 and one of many trips to Yorkshire. Some of my mum's people were up there working at Martin's Farm in Norton, picking fruit on a family estate called Castle Howard. You might have seen *Garfield II* or *Brideshead Revisited*, in which case you will remember the baroque palace which is Castle Howard. It was reached by a long drive that cut through its ornamental gardens, past fountains spilling with Greek gods.

Six miles from the estate was a naturally formed sort of bowl, at the bottom of which was a huddle of derelict red-brick farm buildings, and it was beside these that we pitched up our trailer and car. The milkman refused to deliver the milk all the way down to us each day, and instead used to leave it at the top of the lane that led down to the abandoned farm. I'm not sure whether that was because he was afraid of the creepy buildings, or because we were Gypsies and might read his palm and steal his soul. We liked it well enough down there, though.

One morning I looked up to see the sun flashing through the trees, making the coloured tops of that day's two pints of milk shimmer like reflectors on a bicycle. There were also some lovely horses in a nearby field and, only being around four years old, but thinking myself rather grand and helpful, I took the milk and liberally poured it all into a trough so the horses could drink it.

A nice little treat for them.

I've always loved animals and I thought I was doing good, but the next thing I saw was my mother striding across the field, fixing me with a furious glare and pulling a suitable branch off the hedge so she now had a swishing stick. There's only one purpose for such a stick; she held me with one hand by the top of my ear and repeatedly whipped me on the backside with the other (leaving some very red marks behind). I was screaming like a banshee. She said, 'That's the last time you waste good milk.'

Among the skeletal red-brick buildings, there was a small shed where my older brother Hughie and I once put a goose we'd stolen. We tried to make a little home for it in a box, but then my mother came back from work in the fields and discovered our purloined golden goose, at which point both of us got another good smack. I was about three years old.

Something else bird-related happened there one evening that same summer, something that I will never forget. Remember the barn with the rusty tin roof which my father fell through? Well, on this crooked tumbledown roof, we saw a congregation of blackbirds and crows start to gather. First there was one, then there were three; we blinked and next there were ten, and so it went on – thirty, forty . . . until there must have been over a hundred on the apex of the roof. It was like something out of that Hitchcock film, *The Birds*, with Rod Taylor and Tippi Hedren. It would have been almost comical watching them jostling for space, screaming and cawing like old widows dressed in black, but it wasn't; instead it was odd, wrong.

And as my brother Hughie and I curiously watched them gathering, we saw Mum pause at hanging the washing on the line and stare up at them too. In many cultures, crows are considered agents of the devil and signify bad luck. In Romani lore, my mother's lore, a large collection of black feathered birds signify the coming of death and a predator among us. I felt a chill reach down my young spine and cover my arms in goosebumps. And as they cawed, their black eyes flashing and blinking, the sun was taken by a solitary cloud the size of a battleship and I remembered what they called a huge group of crows: a murder, a murder of crows.

The birds were now no longer cawing but silently watching us, like they had some kind of an agenda and we were a central part of it. My dad appeared, looked to my mother and said, 'Cissy, get me that roll of insulation tape, will you please.' This she did, and Dad wasted no time applying it to the trailer's windows in the shape of crosses across the glass panes, just as the folk in London had during the Blitz, to stop the windows shattering when bombs exploded.

My mother signed herself with the cross and hurriedly pushed us inside the trailer, shutting the door behind her. As we pulled the curtains a crack and peered through the crossed windows, the messengers of doom started their assault on our home. It was as if one of them had given the order for the first crow to dive-bomb us, its wings flush against its body like a feathered missile, beak pointed at the target.

Thud! it came, bruising the side of the trailer, before falling limp to the ground. Then two more, *thud, thud!* Next, it was a free-for-all, and the air was full of their cawing, the flapping of their wings and their talons tearing at the paintwork. Not all of them fell dead on impact with the trailer; many more landed on the roof and began clawing at it, as if they intended to get through the solid metal. I wanted to ask my brother Hughie if he thought that the crosses Dad had put on the windows were to ward off death, or whether it was just to stop them shattering. But even fearless Hughie had gone a lighter shade of pale.

The noise was insufferable; my mother and father were petrified, and Hughie and I were squealing in terror. The attack on the trailer endured for what seemed like an eternity, but was probably more like twenty minutes. And then, as quickly as they had come, they began to disperse; first one or two, then in their dozens and scores. I remember my father saying, 'Give me that towel please.' He started wiping the sweat off his brow and I noticed his hands were shaking.

My parents took themselves into the next room and slid the dividing door shut, but Hughie and I could hear their whisperings as they tried to figure why this murder of crows had visited us. My dad, as I already said, could see around corners, and had this ominous knack of knowing when something bad was about to happen. 'Cissy,' he said, 'something terrible has happened to one of our own.'

The sun might have come out again now, but the atmosphere in the caravan was still as cold as a gravestone. My brother and I sat mute and confused. Within half an hour, we saw a solitary police car rattling down the lane toward us – a navy blue Morris Minor 1000 with a blue light flashing on top. A single policeman climbed out of the car.

'There we go, Cissy,' said Dad to Mum, 'this is what I'm telling you.'

The policeman knocked at the door and my mother opened it. My father stood beside her. The policeman said, 'I'm looking for Cissy and Hughie Burton?'

That was strange, for a start. My dad was so paranoid that he never used his own name, but took my mother's instead. But nobody around here knew us by that name, we had used yet another alias. That could only mean that the police had been contacted by somebody who knew us and had given that name. This was the messenger of doom.

'That's us,' said Dad.

The copper looked at them uncomfortably and said, 'You may want to sit down a moment. Your nephew Owen has just been killed in a car accident, just fifteen miles down the road.'

It was my cousin. At the time the crows had attacked us, Owen had died and met his maker. And though this tragedy marks the end of the story, it began six years earlier, at the start of the sixties, before I was even born.

Owen was hawking with my granny, carrying the carpets, listening to and learning her sales pitch, and saying nothing as he'd been instructed. Granny knocked on a door and a woman peered out and her gaze fell on Owen. Without taking her eyes off him she said, as if in pain, 'I need to tell you something: do not ever take this boy near the coast.'

Granny asked her why and without missing a beat she simply said, 'Because it will be his demise.'

My gran sold her some linen and they left and forgot all about it. The next place they moved on to was called Killamarsh, where there was a big fairground. Owen was watching something on television in his trailer when he lost a clear signal. The trailer was parked up by the side of the road and he took the aerial and moved it around in an attempt to get a stronger signal. As he stepped back a little on to the road, without realizing a car was passing, it hit him. Owen fell over and rubbed his head – he was okay, though. Hearing the screech of car brakes and looking out of the window, one of my aunts saw him sitting up on the side of the road. She ran out in such a rush that she knocked the heater over, which in turn set light to the caravan. Owen cheated death that day.

Fast-forward six years and Owen, who was now seventeen years old, wanted to go to the Appleby horse fair, the biggest annual get-together in the Gypsy diary. But nobody wanted to go with him. His mother finally relented and told him, 'All right, we'll go tomorrow, but first of all I want you to wash and clean the trailer and van. You need to get some Squeezy as we've run out, so pop down the shops first.'

Squeezy – shorthand for washing-up liquid. And so Owen and a couple of friends jumped in a van and drove off, heading toward Bridlington just eight miles away on the coast. En route to the shops, a tractor pulled out, causing Owen to jerk to avoid it, sending the van off the road up a hilly verge. As he swerved violently, one of them was thrown through the windscreen, while Owen fell out of the van's sliding door at the side. As the vehicle fell backwards, it bounced straight on Owen's chest before rolling back down on to the road. One of the boys, on seeing Owen lying there, thought he was okay as there was no blood on him, then ran back home to get help from his dad.

Following the visit by the policeman, we piled in my dad's grey minivan and made our way to where the accident had taken place. At the brow of a hill we saw two little girls walking toward us, sobbing. They were Owen's sisters and, having heard about the tragedy, were now coming to us for help. Six years it had been from when the medium first laid eyes on Owen, to his horrible death, just a short distance from the sea.

Do not ever take this boy near the coast.

*

Come winter, whether we were in Yorkshire, Derbyshire or Nottinghamshire, this was our time for school. Learning was important to my mum. She believed that if we learnt how to read and write we could understand the ways of how 'settled' people lived. So, we went to school not to get A levels and O levels, but to gain an understanding of home dwellers and the way they worked, so we could make our job easier and earn more money from them.

I found school difficult because I didn't go to school regularly, so my education was totally inconsistent. I was suspicious of teachers and so no doubt I came across as difficult and ignorant. Most of the teachers I had seemed to take an instant dislike to me, and a few would make me stand in the corner in front of the class, or tell the other pupils things like, 'John Fury is a Gypsy and he lives on the campsite down the road.' I felt humiliated on a constant basis, and my reaction was to deny that I was a Traveller.

Come home time at 3.45 p.m., the boys in the senior years assembled to fight me. And while I was always more than capable of taking care of myself with people in my year, when the senior lads came at me one after the other, it was hard work. I was about ten years old and had this cheap old watch; I used to rip it out of my pocket and look at it nervously, praying that it was almost four o'clock, which was when my dad used to arrive to pick me up, fifteen minutes after school had ended. You never knew what was going to happen during that period, from when we left the classroom to when Dad would appear in his old grey van, having finished a long day selling carpets. One kid, who was about fourteen years old, tried to do a

Bruce Lee kick on me. Instead I tripped him up with my trusty Doc Martens and kicked him in the face. I jumped on the lad while three others were kicking me in the kidneys.

My dad then appeared, pulled me out of the fray and then gave me a good slap for fighting. I couldn't win! My dad attempted to teach me self-control so I would not let myself get so angry from other boys' taunts. 'Dad,' I'd say, 'you don't like fighting and I respect that, but I feel as if I was born to it and I'm good at it too. When you hit me it doesn't hurt.' From that moment onwards he stopped trying to preach the benefits of being placid and let me go my own way. Many years later, when my son Tyson went to school in Styal, Cheshire, he was huge compared to the other boys in his class. He would often get taunted by older boys, but the difference between Tyson and me was that he learnt self-control and discipline at an early age, and he was better at controlling his red mist.

When I first bought some land, I was in my mid-twenties, and it raised quite a few eyebrows among the Traveller community. It might well be true, as the saying has it, that 'a rolling stone gathers no moss', but to be honest I was tired of moving around relentlessly. The way I saw it, the colliers lived a better life than we did, and I wanted a bit of that. My parents understood the feeling. Despite being on the move a great deal and having caravans as homes, they often said to me, 'Invest in a bit of property, John. Buy some land.' Not that my dad would ever buy a house himself, he loved the freedom of Gypsy life too much, but I think he knew that an era was drawing to a close. Cars were getting quicker and more numerous, and a slow life on the road was getting harder.

The idea of my dropping anchor and setting down roots wasn't typical thinking among our people, and it didn't go down well. A Gypsy back then was like Native Americans once were, before the Pilgrims arrived and they all got locked up and put in reservations; we Gypsies flowed with the seasons and went where the work was, setting up camp beneath the stars. Travellers most certainly didn't stop and build houses.

The reason I had the confidence to buy land and property was all down to some wonderful Travelling people called Mark and Toni White, who were property developers. The Whites were as close as family to us, and owned a couple of caravan parks. They generously taught my brothers and me, when we were very young, how to invest in property. I suppose I looked at Mark and Toni's clothes, their nice house, the fast cars they drove, and thought to myself, 'I want a bit of that.' By comparison, we Furys were a bit raggle-taggle but, despite our material differences, both families got on like a house on fire.

The parish church of Saint Mary's and All Saints in Chesterfield, Derbyshire, has a twisting spire which is famous the world over. Legend has it, the Devil was flying from Nottingham to Sheffield and stopped to rest on the parish church spire. The smell of incense drifting up from

the church below made him sneeze so violently he flew
from the tower, and as his tail caught the top of the spire,
it twisted the structure into its current shape. Doubtless
that old myth got people to church on time, lest the Devil
return. The Furys were certainly God-fearing people, and
this pretty little town with its bent spire and Elizabethan
houses is as close to my heart now as it was back then,
because I grew from a boy to a man in this very place.

There was a caravan park in Chesterfield called Riverdale
Park, owned by a man with one leg called Desmond
Stapleton. I remember him telling my father how he'd
acquired the money to buy the site through compensation
for his missing limb. That was one of the first times I
heard the term 'investment'. To this day, the Stapletons
are still multi-millionaires.

My favourite place in Chesterfield was the cricket club
next door to Riverdale Caravan Park where we stopped for
the winter. There was also a bowls pitch where we'd play
crown green bowls and help to maintain the green. The
cricket club's main draw was a pool table, to which we
quickly became addicted. It was eight shillings (40 pence)
for a pint of lager with a lemonade top. I'd go there with
my brothers and pretend I was drinking straight beer.

My life has been a battle, and I admit I've had so many
fights that most of them I can't remember; but now and
again, memories of these old fights return and it's the ones
I had as a kid that I remember most fondly, as they were
the very essence of me. I loved to fight, but I never insti-

gated it, I just had a habit of being in the wrong place at the right time. For some reason, as I write this morning, I can remember another scrap which happened when I was about thirteen. It was in a place called Jacksdale, somewhere between Chesterfield and Nottingham, and I was hawking, and dressed immaculately in my suit and spit-polished shoes. I knocked on the front door of this terraced house and when this middle-aged lady came out, I began my spiel. She was on the verge of buying a rug off me when her son appeared, announcing that she wasn't going to buy anything as his dad would go mad. He then said something derogatory to me like, 'Get the fuck off my land and take that piece of shit carpet with you before I punch your head in.'

I heard the switch go in my head as my body filled with adrenaline and blood started thundering in my temples; I went from hawking mode to fight mode in a heartbeat. We fought in that lad's front garden for about ten minutes and, I'll be honest, he almost beat me – he was a straight puncher; clearly he'd had some experience fighting – but in the end he gave up before I did. He held his hand up and I said to him, between spitting a glob of blood all over his mother's pruned roses, 'Have you had enough?' and he nodded. Breathless, he held his hand out to me in a gesture of peace and friendship, and I shook it. We were both covered in knuckle marks, with lumpy eggs on our foreheads and black eyes. My nose was cut open, I needed four stitches in the lip and he'd knocked one of my teeth out, but I've never forgotten the fact he wanted to shake hands, and I had tremendous respect for him because of it.

There was something else that day which spurred me on, beyond the indignation of being insulted; I knew my father was parked up waiting for me in the van. All fight long, he had not intervened, he was watching me through its window. Even though my father avoided conflict, I knew that losing a fight in front of him was not an option. All I wanted was for my father to be proud of me. He came from a fighting background, even though he wasn't a fighter himself, and he knew a lot about that world. Many years later when I became a professional boxer, he told me, 'If you're doing it for money, it's a mug's game, and when you get a fighting man's reputation, you'll never have any peace in your life as someone will always be calling you out and challenging you.' And he was so right.

When I walked back to the van (with the carpet in hand), he looked at me and smiled, 'You've a few marks on your face, son,' he said, 'but I'm proud of you, because that boy can fight.'

'I got the win though, didn't I, Dad?'

'Yes, you did, you got the win all right. Let's take the day off.'

I was glowing with contentment.

Another fight comes to mind. I was in Wakefield, a rough rugby league town. It was a cold winter's night and I'd been playing pool in a pub over the road from a chippy and had had a few pints by the time I tried to jump the queue for food. All of a sudden I received a tap on the shoulder, and a deep voice said, 'We're all cold here, mate.'

'I'm a bit late for work,' I lied.

'Get outside!' he snarled. 'Before I put you out.'

'There's no man can put me out,' I answered, all haughty. As if to test the statement, he hit me in the face and I went straight through the chippy's window. He stepped through after me and we had a punch-up outside, amongst the broken glass. People gathered around us in a circle, and I could hear the man's girlfriend crowing, 'Kill him, kill him.'

We gave each other a good hiding, then the police turned up and we were both arrested. He was about twenty-five. I was sixteen.

People often ask me what my most difficult fight was and I answer with little hesitation. Surprisingly, it wasn't against a future world champion, nor was it an underground bare-knuckle fight. I was hawking rugs one day when I knocked on a door on a council estate. An ordinary-looking man, not a big man, about five foot eleven, and around fifteen stone, answered the door. 'What you selling?' he barked.

'Carpets and rugs,' I answered.

'Will any of them fit into my front room?'

'I don't know,' I said.

'I want that one at the bottom of the pile.'

I told him that I wasn't prepared to separate all the rugs and put them on the grass to look at. For a start there was the matter that I was only sixteen, and I didn't have a driver's licence, tax or insurance on the van, nor did I have a hawker's licence. All it would take was some busybody to peer out of a window and assume that the rugs were stolen, then call the police, and I would be in real trouble.

'If you don't unravel that rug, you're not getting off this estate and I'll keep the carpet,' he said. He wasn't interested in the rug, he was just looking for a fight. I told him I was there on my own, trying to make a living, but he was implacable.

'All right,' I said, 'let's fight then. But first, give me a hand to get all of these rugs back in the van.' This we did and then he said, 'Follow me.'

We walked to a nearby deserted playground, where there were a few swings, a slide and one of those spinning roundabouts. We went to straight to it and it was a hard tussle. I lost a tooth and had to have multiple stitches in my lip, while he lost half an ear and was temporarily blind in one eye. He was the son of a pit man and hard as granite. He also knew how to fight.

You can't let this collier beat you, I told myself.

And then, just as I was tiring, he said, 'Enough.'

'Are you beat?' I asked.

'I am,' he said.

I went and sat on the roundabout and began idly pushing myself in slow circles with my foot in an attempt to relax. My whole body was tingling, my nervous system working overtime.

'Are you a Gypsy?' he asked.

'Why do you ask?' I replied.

'Because no regular person can fight like that. Listen, do you want a glass of fizzy pop?'

'Why not?' I said.

'You'll have to drink it outside – sorry, but we're not allowed Gypsies in our houses.'

I took the drink, icy dew gathered on the neck of the refrigerated bottle of Tizer. It tasted like liquid heaven. Drink over, we shook hands and I went on my way, but something was wrong. I was struggling to even put the car into gear as my leg was shaking so badly.

What was going on? I realized adrenaline was flooding my veins and I was shaking at the thought of what a big risk I had taken just to salvage my pride against a rough-mouthed thug. Every moment I remained in the council estate I knew I was inviting a visit from the police. But something else was happening too, that adrenaline was making me feel invincible; I was high on the buzz of what I'd just done. Winning a bare-knuckle fight is the best feeling in the world.

Away from the canvas of the square circle, there is no showboating: you're fighting for your life and the honour of your ancestors and family.

2

From Fighting Stock

Boxing runs deep and dark as Guinness through the veins of a Travelling man. Any self-respecting Gypsy is a fighter; using our fists to settle disputes is as ingrained in us as our love of the horses that draw our wagons, and the songs which warm our hearts around the fire. Machismo and brutish bare-knuckle boxing may be – it's not pretty like the Fancy (the professional fight game) and comes with broken teeth and little style – but it's part of our ways. Away from the canvas of the square circle, there is no showboating: you're fighting for your life and the honour of your ancestors and family.

A Gypsy King is defined as being the best bare-knuckle boxer of all the Travelling people. Bartley Gorman was the last official Gypsy King, and in many ways he belongs to another time. These days, having seen the success and wealth that boxers like Tyson and Billy Joe Saunders accumulated in the pro fight game, most young Travellers would rather go down the same route, so it's unlikely that there will ever be another Gypsy King.

Even an unknown pro boxer just starting out is reasonably well compensated for his time and makes a few thousand quid for stepping into the ring. But Gypsy King or no Gypsy King, there will always be fighting. Drinking and pride are the reasons that people end up with broken noses. When I was younger we would sit around the fire, singing and dancing, and then rip our shirts off and square up to one another.

Bartley Gorman

I first met Bartley Gorman in July 1973. My mother and I had been hawking all day and, when we came back to our wagon, we noticed there was a red MG in the corner of the field and a fire going nearby. Seated next to it was a tall, thin man called Bill Braddock, who wore a fedora hat with a feather in it tilted at a rakish angle, and a broad, thickly set man next to him, who crackled with life. In the fire-glow, his body seemed to be covered in a fine down of hair.

You could have heard them from the next field, they were talking that enthusiastically, and it was all about fighting. The red man was frying some bacon in a pan, which smelt delicious, and when he saw my father, his handsome, broken face lit up with joy and he roared with excitement. Bartley

Gorman was family, my father's cousin. He was also one of the greatest bare-knuckle fighters in recent history. That night I will never forget, as we sat huddled about the flames eating bacon sandwiches on fresh doorstop slabs of bread, drinking and swapping stories. I watched him across the fire; he was enormous and had this huge mop of red hair across his colossal head. *He's a red werewolf,* I thought to myself.

This particular Gypsy King was built with thunder in his fists and a body forged in fire. He was famous for his right hand 'bull hammer' punch, which was aimed right between his opponent's eyes. He could stare down Medusa and live to see the day; even his ginger hair looked like it was made of bronze. But he was the best company you could ever hope to run into; children loved him. He also spoke with a surprisingly quiet, soft voice – it's said that the actor Tom Hardy developed the voice of his character 'Bane' based on Bartley's for *The Dark Knight Rises.*

Bartley loved people and had an unquenchable thirst for life. He was big enough to admit his faults, namely that he loved fighting too much, and was a victim of his own pride. Although being a Gypsy King is indeed the highest title that a Traveller can be lauded with, in those days it came at a cost; every Tom, Dick and Harry wanted to fight him. He couldn't even attend a funeral without someone having a go. The tradition was that a challenger would knock on your trailer at dawn. You had to face every pretender to the crown, or else lose it.

Bartley was a true fighting machine and either he

possessed more valour than Alexander the Great, or – technically speaking – he was stark raving mad, because his courage knew no bounds. He was as happy taking on one man as he was an army; even thirty men all tooled up with iron bars, hammers and broken bottles. I remember exactly this happening in 1976 at the St Leger Day horse races in Doncaster. I was just eleven years old at the time and, being present to watch what was supposed to be a fair fight, I then witnessed a hideous spectacle of such shameful cowardice and brutality it still haunts my memory. The battle of two men against a multitude has now become a story of mythological proportions in Gypsy folklore.

When Bartley and his brother Sam arrived at Doncaster races, the word about the fight taking place that day had been circulating since the day before. They walked across the paddock and saw the broad figure of Hughie Burton walking towards them, with his distinctive blond hair in a ponytail. 'There's a mob waiting for you down there, much too many of them and they'll kill you,' he said. He was an old man now, his mythic fighting days long past.

As Sam and Bartley arrived in the designated place, they looked for the ring they were to fight in, but there was none to be found. At the nearby Park Royal Hotel, the traveller Bartley was due to fight had rounded up a gang of dangerous fighting men to take Bartley and Sam off the board, and they now arrived in an armada of cars and trucks. They jumped from the vehicles carrying iron bars and baseball bats. 'Moment of truth,' Bartley kept saying to himself. 'Moment of truth.'

One of the gang stepped forward and began walking menacingly toward the red werewolf. Bartley hit him so hard that his body left the ground and landed in a heap. Having seen the Gypsy King dismiss their challenger to his crown, without even breaking a sweat (and his opponent was a real force, a fine fighter and the champion of Yorkshire), the gang attempted to save face by tackling him en masse (in full view of the Queen's box). It began with fists, a never-ending wave of man after man gathering like flies around the Gorman boys. Bartley took down the first two, while another of them flew at Sam, but his brother was too quick and strong and struck him down with a single punch. There was just Bartley and his brother Sam, two men against thirty, not exactly a fair fight. Bartley was also a purist, his chosen weapon being his bare hands, and though his fists crashed against many a cranium, cheekbone and nose with the power of a wave splitting the cliffs of Bundoran, he was soon overwhelmed by the numbers. Then scared, the cowardly mob pulled out their iron bars. One hit Sam on the temple, knocking him to the ground. Then they all jumped on in a pile-up, while a man repeatedly kicked Sam in the head. Bartley had ten men hanging onto him. He made for the car and, to his relief, he discovered that Sam had already climbed in the back. No sooner than the Gypsy King was in the Vauxhall, the mob began wrecking the car, teeming over it like ants, smashing the windows.

They dragged Sam from the car, but he tried to hold onto the steering wheel to stop them getting him out into the open, then they put his head under the wheels in the mud in an attempt to get Bartley to accidentally drive over it. Someone smashed the front windscreen, climbed through and, as Bartley passed out, forced an iron bar down his throat, breaking his teeth and severely damaging his Adam's apple. Meanwhile, the opponent he had beaten so easily, now took a broken bottle to his leg and began trying to hack it off as they held Bartley down.

Had it not been for his uncle Peter trying to reason with the pack of dogs, he would've died; however, in the singular moment when they stopped and looked at the old man, Bartley saw his opportunity, turned the key and drove off. In revenge, the mob knocked out every tooth in his uncle's mouth. Cut to ribbons with glass and blade, the Gypsy King nearly lost his life that day, and was in hospital for three months.

Allow me to tell you another story about Bartley, having a ruck with a man called Henry 'The Man Mountain' Quinton. It was in the late 1970s, and Bartley lived in Uttoxeter, which wasn't far from Buxton, Derbyshire, where he had some work to do. 'Do you want to help me out, John?' he asked pleasantly, as ever chipper and all smiles. I agreed without hesitation, Bartley was great to be around and I was around him a lot as a teenager. He was smart, funny, and there was never a dull moment with him. I also knew I could learn a lot from him.

We finished the day's work and I told him I'd best be off back home to where my family were pitched up, and

Bartley said, 'No, stick around, there's a pub I want to take you to, it's like something out of an old Western film, with sawdust on the floor and saloon doors that swing open in the middle.' It was just as he described it. All the talk in the pub that early evening was about a fighting man called Henry Quinton. 'He's as big as Giant Haystacks,' said one. 'He's never been beaten,' said another. Bartley, being a fighting man, was always keen to learn of a new possible opponent, especially one with a reputation.

We were just about to drain our pints and leave when, lo and behold, this huge bear of a man with long claws and a thick beard filled the doorway. Bartley chuckled into his pint. 'I'm thinking that will be "Henry Quinton, The Man Mountain",' he said quietly. This bear of a man was a sight for sore eyes. He looked as if he hadn't washed for months, his clothes were filthy, and he wore a poacher's belt with hooks, on which were impaled various game animals, including rabbits.

He comes to the bar and looks at me. Then his eyes flick to Bartley. 'Who are you?' says Quinton.

'I'm Bartley Gorman, the best fighting man and King of the Gypsies. Who are you?'

'I'm Henry Quinton, I'm a mountain man, I'm the best man around these parts.'

Bartley grinned. 'Yes, you're a fine fella.'

'So are you,' said Quinton.

Bartley's eyes were twinkling, 'Are them rabbits for sale?' he said.

Quinton nodded, 'They are. How many do you want?'

'Give me a couple of them.'

'How do you want them, skinned and ready to go straight into the pot?'

Bartley was intrigued as to how Quinton would deskin an animal in the middle of a pub. 'All right then, if you can, yes please.'

The huge man pulled a rabbit off its hook and proceeded to slit its stomach open with a knife and put his hand in the guts and pull them out. These he swallowed, chased down with a beer.

'I've never seen that done before,' said Bartley, all matter-of-fact.

We then watched Henry Quinton gut another rabbit, this time the intestines were full of shit, and it was all over his mouth and running down his beard as he swallowed that down too. He slammed the rabbit down on the wooden bar top with a menacing finality. 'Is there anything else you want?' he said.

The air in the pub seemed charged with electricity, while outside the sinking sun lingered an instant, lighting up Bartley's coppery hair like fire. 'Yes,' said the Gypsy, 'to fight you! Car park, now, that's where you and me are going. Leave the rabbits here.'

In the next fifteen minutes they went at it hammer and tongs. Quinton, for all his weight and size, was light on his toes and he knew how to box. Bartley had the edge, though; in his mid-forties, he was younger than The

Mountain and a more technically able fighter. He was also fearless. Suddenly, the sound of police sirens filled the air and Bartley yelled, '*Shaydicks!*' meaning 'police' in Traveller gammon (language). We all scarpered.

At fifty-seven years of age, Bartley confided in me that he'd had liver cancer for the last twelve months and, despite his best efforts to ignore it, he knew that his body, a frame that had served him so well, had finally called 'time' – and the bronze titan was heading for his end of days. We took him to the doctor for an X-ray to discover the extent of the cancer, and in complete amazement the doctor said, 'What's this man been doing all his life? I've never seen a body with so many fractures; it's as if he's been dragged along by a four-ton dump truck then driven over! There is not one bone in him that doesn't seem to have been broken at some stage.'

'He's been a prizefighter all his life,' I said.

The doctor explained that the injuries had caused the cancer, and I in turn conveyed all this to Bartley, who just smiled benignly and said, 'Well, that was the profession that I chose and I've loved every minute of it.' He faced death like a man, as did my own father, Hughie Fury. They died within a week of each other, though Bartley was the first to go. Bartley Gorman had made a huge impression on me, so to lose two such important figures in my life within a week of one another seemed a very brutal thing to happen. Life goes on but they're never forgotten, their wisdom and deeds deeply engraved in my memory.

Oathie Burton

Oathie Burton was another fine fighter, and Tyson's grand-father on his mother's side. They say he had the strength of three men, and if he bear-hugged you in affection, you would likely draw your last breath. Even a friendly clap on the back used to send people to the floor. He just had abnormal power. He used to do sit-ups off the back of a lorry and he was always in training, running and shadow-boxing. Wherever he travelled there was always a boxing bag attached to the bough of the nearest tree.

Oathie fought his way through the unofficial ranks until he faced the best boxer in Ireland at the Hook Fair in County Kerry. His opponent had a brother who was also a bare-knuckle boxer. The fight lasted an hour, and as the sun stole across the sky, they traded punches to the face and temple; under the chin, across the jaw, jabs to the stomach, low hooks to the kidneys. And throughout this epic battle, the crowd followed them in an excited procession, as the fighters waded through ditch, stream and meadow until finally Oathie put the man down. His fist was raised to honour him as the new King of the Gypsies. But it wasn't over quite yet . . . early the next morning, fresh as a daisy and ripe for the challenging, the brother of the defeated Irishman knocked on Burton's trailer before dawn as tradition required. Oathie was worn out and bruised but had to pick himself up and fight again. Thankfully his next opponent wasn't as gifted as his elder brother, and Burton was able to bring him down quickly, without much further injury to himself. Afterwards, the father of the two broken boxers was impressed. 'You're very good,' he told him, 'probably the best I've seen, but there's just one problem.'

'What's that?' asked Oathie.

'You're English,' said the man.

Now the Irishman was not the only one with a brother, Oathie had a brother too, who was to become one of the most long-standing Gypsy Kings of them all. Hughie Burton was his name. Where his brother was very bad tempered and easy to coax into battle, Hughie was less easily drawn. Oathie used to say, 'Just hit him if you want to get him fighting – even better, hit him with a stick.' The problem was that once his fire was stoked there was no stopping Hughie, and he would rain down blows on his opponents with such fury and of such a number that anyone who dared fight him was putting their life on the line. Hughie Burton's red mist was more like a pea-souper. In 1960 he fought the best boxer in Scotland and flew into such a rage that he began to bite his opponent's chest off; it was sheeting with blood and the Scotsman rightly pointed out that if any more of him was eaten, he would have to go to hospital or else bleed to death.

Uriah 'Big Just' Burton

Before Bartley Gorman came Uriah 'Big Just' Burton.

Uriah was a lion of a man, and a much-storied figure in

the pantheon of bare-knuckle fighting. They said he could fight two men at once. They say his name was spoken in hushed tones and that he was as strong as a pony. When ponies are in short supply, Gypsies make their money by doing things other people are not prepared to do: one of those jobs was to extract ore from the pits. When Big Just worked the pits, there were no safety helmets and no health-and-safety rules. He would just climb down by a rope and pull out the load by hand, dragging the ore out of the pit tied to his waist. He made a great deal of money and became one of the richest Gypsies in the UK.

Uriah was a handsome, square-jawed man with a shock of thick wavy hair swept back across his broad skull. He wore gold rings on his fingers, sported fine plaid jackets, spoke clear Queen's English and owned Jaguar cars, added to which he was extremely well-read and articulate. He was also uncle to my wife Amber (my son Tyson's mum). Uriah Just was a naturally charismatic leader and people couldn't help but listen to him. Despite his fierce reputation as a bare-knuckle boxer, he threw himself into supporting a peaceful Ireland and, having written a pamphlet about his life, aims and ideals, he is said to have sent it to every global leader in an attempt to sue for a more peaceful earth. With a rich lineage on both my side of the family and his mother's, it's no huge surprise that Tyson is the world champion.

Any boy sent to this type of
institution is a new fish, and
naturally this new fish has to be
tested by the established,
dominant ones in the powerplay.

3

Borstal Bound & On the Run

The past few years had seen me getting in trouble a fair bit; I'd almost reached the crossroads all young men do, as they bid goodbye to their teens and start thinking about what they're going to do with the rest of their life. A man with a plan is a positively dangerous thing, while a teenager without one is only heading in one direction. I didn't have a clue where I was going; the only consistent thing in my life was fighting, which resulted in me ending up in a Borstal – what would now be called a young offenders' institution – at a place called Lowdham Grange in Nottinghamshire.

The idea behind the Borstal system (which began in 1902) was to create a safe place, where the authorities could separate young first-time offenders from seasoned older 'crims' in prisons, who would only teach them yet more antisocial things to do when they got out of clink. These new institutions were designed to give you an education, keep you busy with regular work, and tire your body out with a regime of exercise, whilst instilling in each offender a sense of discipline. The hope was for them to build a skillset so that when their incarceration term was over, these formerly directionless young men would have something to offer the outside world, and could more easily find employment rather than sliding straight back into crime.

Lowdham Grange Borstal first opened its doors in the early 1930s, and the institution's first governor, W. W. Llewellin, was clearly very proud of it. I recently found an essay of his from the 1930s in which Llewellin boasts about the openness of the building and the atmosphere of trust.

Well, maybe it started out like that, and with noble intentions too, but by the 1980s it was more like *Scum*, the brutal 1970s film starring a very young Ray Winston as he becomes the 'daddy' of the institution, thanks to a sock stuffed with snooker balls. At Lowdham Grange there were plenty of locks on doors by now, and there was a surrounding wall. Borstals had become a breeding ground for psychos, sociopaths and bullies, places where young murderers under the age of twenty-one were allowed to integrate with the rest of the reformatory population and prey on harmless young offenders who'd never even seen

46

a 'blade' before, never mind a homemade 'shank'. As soon as I got there I thought, 'I'm *not* staying here.' You see, the worst thing you can do to a Traveller is lock him in a cage. He'll start to disintegrate inside, coming apart flake by flake like a vampire exposed to sunlight.

Any boy sent to this type of institution is a new fish, and naturally this new fish has to be tested by the established, dominant ones in the powerplay, to measure whether he is dangerous and might one day make a play for top boy, or whether he is soft and will just become another number, passively and quietly doing his time. Really, it was no different to a bunch of chimps swinging around in the trees, arguing over who got best share of the bananas and flinging crap at one another. And I wasn't prepared to take crap from *anyone*, be it murderer or thief, top dog or pit bull. I didn't give them time to get to me – unintentionally, as it happened, I took it straight to them.

During the first couple of weeks, I noticed a ginger-haired lad whose name was Simon who was small for his age. His life was being made a misery by a couple of boys who kept on at him mentally and physically, wearing him down with their bullying. They just wouldn't let up. One day, I found them picking on him in the dormitory. Empty places, like school corridors during lessons, or abandoned buildings, they are spaces in which bullying flourishes and takes root. There wasn't a soul in the dormitory but for these three lads – two against one (or more like two against one half, as Simon was tiny).

It didn't take much thinking about, but before I stepped in I was clear enough that I *did* have a choice; namely, that I could look the other way and pretend I wasn't there, then tiptoe silently out of that spartan wood-floored dorm, or I could do what John Fury had been doing all his life, and stick up for the underdog. I was never one to take a back step, not then, not before, and not ever since. I strode into the room and all six foot three inches and sixteen-plus stone of me alerted them to my presence. One of them with a weasel face looked back at me and nodded to his friend. Simon looked at me as if I was the second coming, his freckled face apologetic about what he knew I was about to drag myself into.

I told his tormentors to leave him be and, like a couple of hyenas disengaging from a carcass, they left Simon and instead made their way towards me. I punched the first weasel so hard that his nose shattered and he was left clutching it, looking in disbelief as it dripped crimson through his fingers, creating a pool of his own blood on the floor.

My mind was racing, my heart pumping with panic, sending adrenaline through my body. A single sentence flashed clear as neon in my mind as I looked at each entrance or exit in the dorm. 'Get out *N-O-W!*' it screamed. I knew I would be in huge trouble for this act of violence, and I was sure they would send me to a closed prison, add another ten years to my sentence and then throw away the key.

The other bully had run off, either to tell a staff member

or, more likely, to seek backup to stem this one-man Gypsy rebellion. I wasn't interested in their crown. We left the boy out of earshot and I said to Simon, 'I've gotta get out of here right now!'

'I'm coming too,' he said.

'It's easier if I go on my tod,' I said.

But Simon convinced me to let him come along, on the basis that he knew the area really well and he could help me escape.

Then it started to rain.

Each boy at Borstal belonged to a house, ours being Stansfield House. I looked out of the three-storey window, across the trimmed lawns at the surrounding fields and sodium-orange glow of Nottingham, no more than five miles away. Then I looked down at the balconies below projecting outward; I'd have to jump well clear of them if I wasn't going to break my neck. My stomach lurched. But I was more petrified at the prospect of being locked up for the next ten years; I just couldn't bear the thought of growing old behind bars. I thought of that French convict in the film *Papillon*. He was called Henri Charrière and was wrongly convicted to serve life in prison for the murder of a pimp in Paris. They sent him to the penal colonies of French Guiana and he kept escaping. Steve McQueen had played him in the film. Unlike Charrière, we didn't need to jump from a cliff to escape from Devil's Island on a raft made of coconuts, we just had to leg it miles to Simon's house. But we did need to jump.

I took a deep breath and, from the top floor of Stanfield House, I propelled myself outwards into the falling rain. It may have been July but, thankfully, the flowerbeds had been frequently watered with a hosepipe by one of the inmates, and so had not been allowed to bake hard. I landed in the middle of a rose bed. So far so good.

As I sought cover in a bush, something went crack on my back. Simon had also aimed for the rose bed, but hadn't waited for me to move, and had now landed splat on top of me with his knee. It should've hurt like hell, and doubtless would later on if we were caught, or had made good our escape, but right now I had so much adrenaline running through me that all I could think about was getting out of Lowdham Grange. For ever. I knew it was the kind of place where you could spiral into further trouble. At the time, the Conservative government was calling Borstal a 'short sharp shock'. Well, it was that and more. Some kids lived in fear, and it wasn't just the prospect of taking a hiding from an older boy. The screws at some of these places were disgraceful too; they seemed to be allowed to punch inmates for any minor insubordination, while sexual predators among the staff were allegedly free to abuse whoever they wished with impunity. I use the term 'allegedly', as in the short time I was in the Borstal system I personally was never subjected to it. But sorry stories are now coming out in the present day, as victims who were detained in these centres in the 1970s and 1980s are finally beginning to come forward to disclose what they were subjected to, and have tried to bury all their adult life. As some of us know, you can't keep a dark secret like that down; it will contaminate your mind for the rest of your days.

I noticed in the short time I was there that some kids were routinely beaten for nothing at all. Sometimes, it might have been they had forgotten to say 'sir' when answering one of the staff. Also, many of the offences that kids were sent down for would never have merited prison sentences today, like shoplifting or receiving stolen goods. The facts are now emerging that the 'short sharp shock' was a complete failure, as many ex-Borstal lads slid into deeper career crime on release because they had been dehumanized by the system, while others suffered terrible mental illness after their experiences, which drove them to drug and alcohol addiction. I cannot imagine how many suicides there were in these places, but I'm sure the figure was high.

He may have been small, but Simon was a good runner and, true to his word, he seemed to know his way around these parts. Suddenly, a piercing wail of police sirens alerted us to the fact that our flight from the Borstal had become common knowledge. The cops were involved now. As the rain fell in biblical quantities, Simon led us to a farm where we found a shed to hide in and wait for the dark. Magically, we hadn't been found yet, and twilight was now losing an arm wrestle with the coming night. The only time that I allowed myself to relax a little was when it was properly dark. 'What's the plan?' I asked Simon.

'We'll head to my house about five miles away. Then we'll change out of these clothes. You can have some of my older brother's. You're bigger than him and they might look a bit short, but it will be better than what we've got on.'

It could have been almost comical if it had been someone else's life I'd been watching. I looked at our striped shirts, beige trousers and black shoes; our Borstal uniform felt like it was burning holes in my skin.

'Ready?' he said. I nodded. We put our heads down and ran like boys on fire, leaping fences, scaling barbed wire, passing through people's back gardens, only ever stopping to catch a breath. At one point, running through an alley, I knocked over a metal bin that clanged loudly. But finally, soaking wet, we came to a back garden where Simon paused. 'This is my house,' he said. 'And don't worry, my mum is sound.'

'What about your dad?' I asked.

'He'll be in the pub.' He went in the back door to the kitchen and beckoned me to follow. His mum looked at us; we must have looked like two bereft waifs. 'Come in, you poor things, you're soaked.'

Simon said, 'This is my mate John, Mum, we've escaped, we've had enough.'

His mum was a lovely gentle person, as was his sister. She looked at me and said, 'What do you need, John?'

'I need some dry clothes, please.'

She smiled. 'Well, I'm not sure we've got anything that

will fit you, but we'll see what we can do.' Simon's sister returned with a shirt and proceeded to cut the arms off it at the shoulder, and then she found me a jumper. All changed, and looking better than I had, I decided my best bet was to leave Nottingham as soon as could be. I'd call my family – not my dad, though, as he would take me straight back to the institution. Instead I rang my brother Jimmy, via the operator, who reversed the charge of the call to my brother. He was about thirty miles away in Chesterfield and he soon made his way over in a Ford Fiesta van. 'What are you going to do?' he asked.

'Take me to South Wales,' I said. My brother Hughie was also in the car and he chimed in. 'I'm coming with you, I'm on the run too.' Hughie had failed to turn up to a court hearing but had jumped bail. The only one who wasn't a fugitive in that Fiesta van was Jimmy, however, at fifteen years of age, he was an underage driver. 'Take us to Aunt Winnie in South Wales,' I said.

'But Dad will kill us,' he protested.

'Never mind Dad, this is bigger than him. I seriously hurt a man in Borstal, and if I go back I'm looking at ten years.'

Aunt Winnie was my dad's oldest sister and sound as a pound. Like my granny she was wise as anything, and could get you out of all sorts of trouble. My brother Hughie suggested we contact our parents, or at least get word to them that we were okay, before news reached them of my escape, so we called up Des Stapleton, the one-legged owner of the campsite they were parked up on, and gave him the following message. 'John, Jimmy and Hughie all fine and on our way to Winnie's.' Only my dad would know where Winnie was.

The sirens had stopped wailing by now. The police would have widened their search, I figured, looking further afield for two teenagers in flight, perhaps in the next county? Hughie looked at my clothes. 'What *are* you wearing?' he laughed.

When we arrived at the field in Merthyr Tydfil where Aunt Winnie's trailer was parked, my heart leapt in my mouth as I spotted my dad's car. I thought, *here we go, I've got some serious explaining to do.* They were all there, waiting for us – my aunt, all the boys, my dad. Contrary to what I thought was going to happen, everybody made a grand fuss of us. They fed us lovely food and even went to the shops to get us some new clothes to wear. My dad asked me, 'Why did you do it, son?'

'I had a fight with somebody, they were gonna give me another ten years.'

'But what exactly did you do to this boy?'

'Broke his nose, Dad.'

He shook his head. 'You idiot! You don't get ten years for breaking somebody's bleeding nose in a Borstal, though you may get ten years for running away.'

For the next two days he tried to reason with me and get me to hand myself in. 'You'll always be on the run, you'll never get bail. Now what kind of a life is that?' he asked.

I thought about those idiots in the dorm, and I wondered if Simon was all right . . . there was no way I was jumping out of that third-storey window again. 'I'm not going back,' I said resolutely.

'Me neither,' added Hughie.

So Father let us be, for better or worse, to make our own decisions. It must've been hard for him to let go of his authority. I suppose he believed we had now reached an age where we needed to think for ourselves and learn by our own mistakes. As it turned out, things weren't half bad for Hughie and me. That summer we worked with my cousins, Tarmacking around Merthyr Tydfil, moving on through the stunning Brecon Beacons and then pushing west into Carmarthenshire. I had my own trailer, and some nights we'd drive with my cousin in his new Mercedes to local discos.

It was a great summer, but even great summers must finally die to make way for the melancholy season of autumn. Out of nowhere my dad appeared like an emissary of the changing season and, with a tone of finality, he said, 'You are going to have to turn yourself in.'

'I'm not going to do that, Dad.'

'Your cousins are all going back to Doncaster for the winter, how are you going to get home?'

'It's not home any more,' I said. 'Home is at the front of this trailer. I'll see where it takes me, take my chances. I've got a few quid put away. I'll set something up.'

I decided on Yorkshire. I'd find a city there large enough

to lose myself in, a place I could effectively disappear while doing the odd bit of work.

I met my future wife Amber at this time, and she was a real head turner. I had first seen her when I was about twelve at the Doncaster races, then again three years later, and finally now as an eighteen-year-old. She was a stunner. A short time after we met, Amber fell pregnant with John Boy. Financially, things were tough for us from the word go. I had an old trailer and car, and barely a fiver in my pocket. My prospects weren't good; every time I saw a policeman, or heard a dog bark or a bird sing, I anticipated the police kicking down my door. I was close to suffering a nervous breakdown with the constant anxiety. I could hardly support myself, never mind a new baby.

Outside the window of the trailer, I saw a familiar face. It was Frank, Amber's brother. He had been looking for me for the last few months. His van was full of carpet, he was doing well and had money in his pocket. 'Frank,' I said, 'you are a lifesaver. Things have been hard of late. Now, let's go to Bradford and sell all those carpets before the end of the day.'

We made about £400 each that day, and from having nothing in my pocket to then have it bulging with a fat wad of cash felt good. Frank said, 'I know some good metal places in Bradford.' We did some good business selling scrap for a few days. One day we got sloppy and overloaded the van with scrap metal. Frank pointed to one of the van's tyres and said we needed to fill it up. We stopped at a garage for the air-machine, but it was broken. Some things are just written in stone up there, aren't they? Shortly after, going round a roundabout, the tyre – overloaded with the pressure on it – burst, and the van tipped over. Frank nearly broke his neck, I hit my head and knocked myself out on the side of the road, while all the metal flew every-where. When I came to, I was feeling decidedly out of it.

It wasn't long before the police arrived.

'Uh-oh, here come the *muskers*,' said Frank.

'You all right, lad?' asked the copper.

'Yes, I think so,' I answered.

'What's your name?

'Peter White,' I said.

Frank gave his own name. Why I was driving I have no idea, given that he had a licence and I didn't. The policeman said, 'What have you got in the back of the van?'

'Scrap,' I answered.

'Okay, Peter White, do you have any identification?'

'No, but he has,' I answered, pointing at Frank.

He took a long hard look at the both of us – particularly me – and said, 'Something about you isn't right, Mr White. I'm arresting you both on suspicion that you're wanted.'

The smile fell off my face. *How can he possibly know!*

The upshot was, he wanted my fingerprints.

'I don't want to give you my fingerprints as that would make me a criminal, and I'm not a criminal.'

He wasn't a mean man; he looked at me and smiled. 'All I'm going to do is take your prints, run them through the system to make sure you are who you say you are and don't have any skeletons in the closet, and then – all being good – you can go.'

'Okay,' I bluffed. 'Take my prints, I've got nothing to hide.'

After sitting in a nondescript room for hours, the prints came back as negative. I tried to hide the expression of relief from my face as the policeman apologized for taking up my time. Next thing, I was at the counter getting my things back, and just about ready to leave the police station and return to my wife and little baby, when this man walked past me and stopped dead behind me. I could feel his eyes burning holes in the back of my neck. 'Turn around,' he said.

In my defence, the kindly copper walked over and said, 'He's okay. He's called Peter White, and he's not on the system, no priors whatsoever.'

The other man wasn't convinced. 'I've seen this man before. He's wanted.'

I spoke up, 'I'm not wanted. I've done nothing wrong.'

This time I was detained in a little glass room. The minutes ticked by. Ten became fifteen and then it was half an hour . . . tick-tock, tick-tock . . . my pulse began to race. After forty-five minutes, my accuser opened the door. In his hand he carried a poster. He unscrolled it. 'Who's that?' he said, poking at it with his finger.

'I've no idea,' I said.

'Really? Well, let me tell you. It's John Fury, and that's

who you are, lad. Look, it's been almost three years since you escaped. You've committed no offences whilst on the run, so things can only get better for you. You're going to have to return to the system before you can get your life in order again. The reason I know who you are is because I'm on the force in Nottingham and we often scratch our heads and say, "I wonder where the hell John Fury's got to?"' He laughed and said, 'I'll tell you one thing, you're a star fugitive!'

What are the chances I'd be spotted by a passing copper from Nottingham? I thought to myself.

I told him about having a young wife and a newborn baby to support, and how my life had gone down the toilet. He was sympathetic and offered to try and make a bid for a shorter term for me, based on my cooperation. 'But I'm afraid it won't be an open place like Lowdham Grange. You'll be in an enclosed Borstal this time.'

'Can I make a confession?' I asked. 'The reason I escaped was I had a fight with a lad and gave him a bit of a hiding, and I think I injured him.'

'Injured him how?'

'I broke his nose.'

'You became a fugitive because you broke someone's nose? I don't care if you broke his jaw or his skull, you shouldn't have run away. But nothing's been reported so forget about it.'

I finished my time in a prison in Leicester called Glen Parva, one of the roughest closed-cell prisons for young offenders. There was a lot of violence there. I did what I had to do to survive, but largely I kept my nose clean and I was out within nine months. By the time I got out, John boy was already fourteen months old. All I wanted now was to get on with my life, raise a family and keep on the right side of the law. It would be another thirty years before I spent more time at Her Majesty's Pleasure.

Tyson is a very different character
to me, but in the ring I see the
same warrior instinct coming out
that was once displayed
by his ancestral Gypsy Kings;
he's completely fearless.

4

The Coming of Mr Hyde

The horror writer Edgar Allan Poe once wrote that the scariest monsters are the ones that live inside our souls. As I grew older, it became clear to me that someone else shared the twisting corridors in my mind, and it wasn't somebody I liked. I get my temper from my mother and, as you'll read over the coming chapters, it hasn't helped me in life; in fact, quite the opposite, as that inability to control myself has landed me in some very dark places, which could've easily been avoided.

I lose my temper when somebody insults me or my family, or when I'm presented with cheek or dishonesty. Violent thoughts fill my head, I hear a thundering in my temples, feel the blood galloping through my veins and I become possessed by this strange, raging force within me.

Mr Hyde kicks down the door of my self-control and comes stamping down the corridor with a strange light in his eyes. Like a pit bull, he doesn't know how to back down. After the furious flames and hideous violence, Hyde retreats darkly back to his hut until the next time, and Doctor Jekyll comes to, and I look around at the physical devastation my fists and teeth have caused another human being, then sadly shake my head.

Even now in my late fifties, my dark half still haunts me, and because of it I have become something of a recluse. I realize how close I walk the razor's edge every day of my life, and I have to be extra careful of the situations I place myself in. I avoid crowds, funerals, weddings, in fact any social scene wherever there's men and drink, that could be a potential banana skin on which to slip and end up back in jail.

I can remember the day I first became aware that I was as powerless against this darkness as a weatherman is against a mighty tornado. My dad had sent me down to the nearest shop to get him some cigarettes, and my little brother Peter had asked if he could come with me. 'Yes,' I told him.

'And can we get some sweets?' he said.

'Yes, course we can, provided that's all right with Dad,' I answered.

We'd had trouble with some pit boys a few weeks earlier, me and my older brother Hughie, and I spotted them and pointed them out to Peter, but as we now came around the corner past the post office, I realized the group was in fact four men in their thirties leaning on a wall. They looked like trouble, and their heads snapped up when they saw us, almost as if they had been waiting for us. One looked very familiar, just like one of the pit lads we had a problem with, only now he looked like he'd grown a beard and added a few years.

Surely those big grown-up men, they're not going to pick a fight with a fifteen-year-old and his twelve-year-old brother, I thought to myself.

We went into the shop and I bought some cigarettes, and from the change I got some sweets for the 'baby' (that's what we used to call Peter, since he was the youngest). As we were about to leave the shop and walk outside, I noticed my brother was deathly pale, the colour drained from his cheeks. He knew what was coming, that the men intended to give us a beating, and yes it must have been scary for him, very scary. The air felt hot to touch, electrically charged with impending violence. In my stomach I felt a building anger that these men might be looking to set their fists loose on a twelve-year-old. It was wrong.

I took Peter by the shoulders, bent down and said slowly, 'What you need to do now is run straight home and tell Hughie to come on his own to help me.' Now, Hughie was only sixteen, a year older than myself, but I figured having him there would even the odds up a little bit.

As we left the shop, one of the men leaning on the wall, a brute with a beard on him, said, 'Hey gyppo, you hit my little brother the other week.'

No wonder he was familiar, it was the pit lad's dad.

I turned to him and said, 'Yes I did, and I'll hit him again today if you like?'

'No, you're fighting me today.' Pushing himself up from the wall.

'You're a little bit old for me, my old mate,' I replied. 'But if I've got to fight you, I've got to fight you.'

I looked behind me to check Peter had left to get Hughie, but he was still there.

'You run!' I shouted, jabbing my finger at him. He shook his head, the expression on his face now one of steely intent, the colour almost returned to his cheeks. 'No, I'm not running,' he said quietly.

The man with the beard wasted no more time with words; he was moving straight for me. I hit him with a left and a right; he went straight down and I kicked him full in the face with the instep of my hobnailed boots. Meanwhile, one of the other men had gone for Peter, whose instincts had kicked in, and he peppered his opponent in punches, bop, bop, bop, and then he went down too. A twelve-year-old boy had flattened a man who must have been twenty-eight years old.

I wasn't finished. Possessed by rage, I jumped on top of him, and bit the top of his eyebrow and then his ear. It was as if a monster had been released within me, and – not content with the handiwork of its claws – it was now baring its teeth. As with every fight I'd ever had, someone else had started it, but I had finished it on my terms. It had been the first time I had experienced fear; not the kind of fear that sends you running in fright, but a fear of the unknown, of fighting a man twice my age. And it had been easy. Admittedly, physically he wasn't much of a challenge, standing at five foot ten and weighing about twelve and a half stone.

I looked at the other men. 'I'm finished with him. Which one of you wants to go next?'

None of them were prepared to take the risk.

After this incident, I felt a kind of armour forming around me, a sense of invincibility that I could not be beaten by another man. I set to work on the weights to build muscle and started running to get fit. I had been fighting most of my life and I realized I enjoyed it and was naturally good at it. Most people faced with the prospect of violence experience a crippling sense of dread and avoid confrontation. Instead of this, I have a switch that gets flicked and I can't walk away.

It's only later, after I have gained some distance from the violence, that I start to go through in my mind all the reasons why I shouldn't fight. Why can I not just walk away and avoid trouble when it comes knocking at my door? It has been seven years since I went to prison for the last time, and there were lessons I certainly learnt from while I was inside. Life is fragile, life is short, and you can so easily throw it all away. I was lucky, I had a second break and I got to live my life again, one which surrounds me with the love of my family. But now, in my later years,

I still sometimes feel like I'm at war with myself, still needing to avoid an altercation that might be waiting for me. I'm a one-strike lifer – any more problems from me and the 'powers that be' have warned me very clearly that I'll be getting twenty-five years to life. Game over. I'm considered borderline dangerous by the authorities. Whereas I believe that dangerous people are very different: they're not family men, they don't look after their kids, and they don't respect other people.

I've been to jail three times in my life – the first, that brief spell at Borstal before I escaped, the second when I finally did my owed Borstal time at Glen Parva, almost three years later; and finally, I served four years of an eleven-year sentence, which was commuted for good behaviour, first at Strangeways, and later at an open prison. As I said to my barrister the last time I went to prison in 2011, 'I'm only dangerous to people who provoke me and bring the fight to me.' Things can go from bad to worse in prison. Prisons are full of desperate men, many of whom have given up and have nothing to lose. Trying to be well behaved and keep your head down is not easy.

I've always given the other person an out and warned them, 'Listen pal, this is your chance to walk away from this because, once I go, I'm not in control of my head, and if you don't get the better of me, I'll be right on top of you and then it's over for you.'

At press conferences and weigh-ins for boxing matches, you could say that there's a lot of theatre going on; fighters act a good game of trash-talking their opponent and what they're going to do to them. But for me, I'm afraid it's not acting; I get genuinely mad. When somebody is openly disrespectful to my sons or to me, the switch is flicked. It doesn't seem to matter how old I am, I can't get rid of it.

After a life spent fighting, I can understand and read truly violent men; I know only too well by looking at a man's eyes whether he is pretending to be angry or is really ready to go for it. There are giveaways in body language, eyes, demeanour and tone. Personally, I have no fear of anyone, whether it's Deontay Wilder or David Haye that gets my goat. I may be an old man in boxing years, but I still run thirty miles a week, and I am still in the gym training my boys and keeping myself fighting fit. The last thing that a fighting man loses is his will to win, and I can do a lot of damage in the space of two minutes. Not that I would want to, but that I know I can.

My mother used to say to us kids, 'Don't let nobody put you down. Don't let anybody say something to you and let them get away with it. On all occasions, if they try to take the mickey out of you and make you look small, you fight, and when you fight you give your all.' Problem with this is that I suppose it's hardwired into me. Tommy Miller, the old boxing coach and promoter, used to say to me, 'You've been punched and hit all your life, whereas many fighters in the ring have barely been in a fight outside the ring, without gloves on. They don't know the ferocity or the magnitude of problems that can occur from a fist fight and its severity.'

When people meet me, they find to their surprise that they are talking to a person with good manners, a softly spoken voice, and somebody who treats others with respect. I'm helpful and caring toward others, and nothing like I appear to be on YouTube videos, which sensationalize me losing my temper. But some naive individuals mistake kindness for weakness. They think they can be disrespectful and make themselves feel more of a man by talking rudely to me. The next thing they know they're spark out cold on the floor, a towel on their head and somebody with smelling salts trying to wake them up.

Tyson, and in fact all my boys, know full well if I'm on my own and one of these idiots gets under my skin and tries to rile on me, then it's all over, I'll be going back to jail. From a young age, they've been able to see what's coming, have a gentle word in my ear and say, 'Dad, back off, it's not worth it.' At the Fury vs Francesco Pianeta weigh-in in Belfast in 2018, Deontay Wilder was in the wings cussing us and my switch was flicked. The audience was roaring 'Fury! Fury!' and savouring the theatre of the moment, encouraging a scuffle to break out. I was on the side of the stage, bending down and jabbing my finger at Wilder's face. Ben Davison, Tyson's then coach, did his best to prise me away from the trouble that was about to erupt, and even Tyson had to intervene with a few quiet words to me. He could see the change come over me, that my mind had gone and I was going to jump on Wilder.

The boys grew up seeing me fight. Sometimes 'heavies'

sent to extort money from me came to the door; it was always a couple of men they sent where I was concerned, as any less and they wouldn't stand a chance against me. My boys they'd say, 'Is it kicking off, Dad? Can we watch?' and I'd reply, 'You can, but stay indoors whatever happens, stay where you are, and watch through the window.'

Speaking of windows, I once had a couple of cowboys put some windows in for me and they did a real duff job, the rain was leaking in, and they tried to charge me four thousand quid for the job. I said, 'I'm not paying for them until you come back and fix them.'

'Oh I think you will,' said one of them with a smirk.

So they sent the heavy mob in. A couple of juiceheads appeared down my lane in a new white 750 BMW. You know the type, typical weightlifters who can't put their arms flat against their sides because they're pumped up with so many anabolic steroids. They have wicked tempers, and their privates have shrunk as a side effect of the drugs. I went out to meet them, stood my ground, didn't flinch, and smiled at them as they climbed out of the car, these three deluded bouncer types. *This will be fun*, I thought, *I'll save myself four grand . . . easy work.*

And so it was. *Bing, bang, wallop,* a battle royal!

As the first one came towards me, I knocked him straight out with a left hook. The next came from the back seat of the car and he received a headbutt to the face for his troubles. The third steroid monkey came from nowhere and jumped on my back, knocking me off balance. I fell to the floor with his weight on top of me, but then I turned him around and had him for breakfast. The only thing that got out of there that morning without a scratch on was the BMW, though there must have been some blood on it somewhere. Juiceheads are shabby fighters; they have no speed or coordination, all bark and no bite. I almost felt sorry for them as they picked themselves off the floor and hurriedly squeezed themselves back into that German car and drove away. At six foot three and twenty stone, I have always stuck up for the wronged, the weak, for myself and my family. I've never felt the need to use a gun or a knife; for me that is cowardly. The only two weapons I've consistently needed are my fists, and my morality map has always been the Bible.

Tyson is a very different character to me, but in the ring I see the same warrior instinct coming out that was once displayed by his ancestral Gypsy Kings; he's completely fearless. The difference between us being that Tyson is in complete control of his fists and his faculties, whereas – when I let rip – I'm not. My mum used to say, 'Of all my sons, I worry about my John the most because he can't keep control of himself. I've watched him when he turns irate and he becomes another person. You never know how far he's going to go with it.'

Tyson was such a unique talent as he grew up. I believe he thought he could get on better with someone else other than me handling his career and coaching him when he turned professional. Perhaps he wanted that independence.

No matter who trains Tyson, it took what was inside me to create a world heavyweight champion. I never give up, at least not while I'm conscious and my body parts are working, and that's where Tyson gets that tenacity. I've always engaged with a mindset that if I am going into battle, anything will go in order for me to get that win. There can be no half measures; you've got to be all-in as a fighting man.

The trouble is that when the red mist descends on me, consequences are no longer on my radar, and my opponent doesn't stand much chance of stopping me. If you are in an organized bare-knuckle fight, you bear no grudge against your opponent – you're both there to beat hell out of one another and one of you is going to win, end of. But if an argument breaks out with somebody where there is a previous history of hate and pride, it can very quickly spiral out of control.

Years ago, I ended up losing my temper in a pool hall. I'd spent weeks tracking this guy down who owed me money. I said to him, 'You've got my money, it's time to pay me back.'

'The only thing you're going to get from me is a good hiding,' he answered.

I looked at him and shook my head. 'Look, you don't know what you're dealing with, you're not in my class. Give me the money you owe me so I can walk out that door, otherwise you're in trouble.'

The man in the pool room threw a straight shot at me,

and the next thing happening in his world was that his head was being banged repeatedly on the wood-veneered edge of the pool table, the overhead light swinging violently, blood discolouring the royal blue felt a deep purple. I was aware of muffled voices, they seemed a long way away, as if they were at the end of a tunnel, telling me to stop. Then they jumped on me, perhaps ten people pinning me down. The man was stretchered away while I, thanks to the no-holds-barred contribution of Mr Hyde, was picked up in a police van before being carted off to jail to ruminate on my actions behind bars. In the aftermath of this violence, I felt an overwhelming sense of shame and contrition. *How could you do that to this man?* I'd ask myself over and over again.

Every time I've ever been to court for fighting with another man, I have always accepted my guilt and never entered a plea of innocence. And though these instances have landed me in such deep water, not one of them was started by me. Without exception, it's been a case of somebody owing me money or darkening the family name, and that has left me no other option than to respond the best way I know how.

———————

Things are gradually getting

easier in terms of discrimination,

but we're still a long way from

where we need to be.

———————

5

Understanding Travellers

My mother was Romani and my father from Irish Traveller stock. Romani Gypsies, also known as Sinti, Roma or Kale, originally came from the Punjab region of northern India, where they were first recorded as early as the eighth century. Their language was Romani. They didn't reach Britain until 1515. The word 'Gypsy' comes from the fact that people thought they'd come from Egypt. In the fourteenth century they migrated through the Balkans into Greece, settling in Corfu. In the 1500s there are records of the Roma people being welcomed to royal courts, where they were thought of as exotic novelties and paid for their ability to tell fortunes and play music – as minstrels and storytellers, knife grinders and hawkers.

The first anti-Gypsy laws appeared in England in 1530,

with the 'Egyptians Act', which essentially banned the Romani from entering Britain. Shortly after they were banned in Moravia and the area now known as Czechoslovakia, and in what was later to become Germany, it wasn't considered a crime to kill a Gypsy. Why did things change for them so dramatically? Probably because they're outsiders, and as free spirits and gifted people they are often misunderstood. In the eighteenth century the wandering lifestyle almost came to an end when travel among Romani was banned and children were taken away.

The Romani have been persecuted for as long as anyone remembers, and it's often overlooked just how many Gypsies were murdered in the Nazi gas chambers or died of starvation in concentration camps like Belsen and Auschwitz. Twenty-five per cent of European Romani perished in the genocide. In 1939 Gypsies lived in Germany, Romania, Hungary, Yugoslavia, Czechoslovakia, Bulgaria and the Soviet Union. *Zigeuner* is the German word for Gypsy and comes from a Greek word meaning 'untouchable'. Given Hitler's obsession about blond and blue-eyed people representing the true sons and daughters of the Fatherland, Gypsies – with their swarthy dark looks – didn't stand a chance. The purity of German blood was to be protected at all costs, and a means of identification was created so they knew who to target. It was called 'racial hygiene'. Gypsies were identified by the Nazi government as a social nuisance, and many were sterilized so they were unable to give birth. The reason? Once again, they were all deemed to be criminals.

Modern-day Irish Travellers were nomadic (though many had smallholdings) and kept themselves to themselves; but though they had clairvoyant gifts and a celebrated folklore, they were not related to the Romani and came from pure Irish stock. Their DNA is 100 per cent homegrown in Ireland, and they can proudly trace their history back to the 1100s. As a distinct medieval group, they predate the Romani in Ireland, who would not arrive there until 200 years later. After this time, the two bloodlines naturally mixed because of their nomadic lifestyles. I am half Romani and half Traveller.

From the start, Travellers were known for their skills making jewellery and ornaments, and because they were tinsmiths they also earned the name 'Tinkers'; so it was actually a compliment. Another name for them was the 'Walking People'. As they moved from place to place, they sold animals and handmade crafts, as well as helping out on farms as casual labour, and in the building trade. Travellers today, like their medieval forebears, are cele-brated for their musical gifts both as fiddlers, singers and on *uilleann* pipes, and of course for their natural ability as storytellers.

The UK is home to approximately 60,000 Travellers, most of whom live in Ireland.

Our history is sometimes a bit vague, because there are no official records written down about us. Everything is handed down through the oral tradition, from our customs to our rich history. Since our ways are different, we tend to arouse suspicion and misunderstanding in regular communities. And because of the way that we've been treated in the past, we tend to look on house dwellers with suspicion, keeping ourselves to ourselves. It's understandable when you look back at some of the history; in the 1600s it was an offence just to talk to a Gypsy.

Travellers fared better when they were permitted to move around in the countryside, away from urban areas. We were better integrated into society until the early 1960s, when a new law referring to us as 'itinerants' tried to make us settle down in one place. Why the nomadic lifestyle was such a problem to the British establishment, I know not, but trying to cage a bird against its will and forcing people off small campsites to live in council houses or council-run campsites was not a great move. While I opted to bring my family up in a house I rebuilt with my own hands, I am through and through a Gypsy and a Traveller.

Some say we were farmers until Oliver Cromwell invaded Ireland, seized our land, made us homeless and forced us onto the road, living by our wits. But to say that we weren't on the road beforehand is not true. Selling our wares and moving from place to place was what we always did; if we'd stayed in the same place, local people would have bought all we had to sell and have no further need of our goods.

Things are gradually getting easier in terms of discrimination, but we're still a long way from where we need to be. One of the reasons for this is that Traveller folk are

The Fury family in the late 1930s parked up in Cheltenham. The man on the left in the suit is my grandfather, his brother is in the suit on the left with their kids in front.

My grandparents on my mother's side, Philip and Louisa Skeet.

This is my father next to his Bedford J type truck, 1968. He loved to dress up.

On the left is my aunty Rose and on the right is my mother, aged seven. At Potters Farm in Kent.

My christening day.
I was eight days old and
held by my father Hughie.

Me on the right at eighteen
months old with my eldest brother
Hughie at the races, 1967.

Me on the left, eighteen months old,
sat next to Hughie.

Me at three years old, my newborn
brother Peter is in the pram.
This would have been taken in
Dewsbury, Yorkshire, 1968.

Me on the left at five years old with my brother Hughie in Derby, 1970. Next to us is our caravan.

Me and my three brothers, Burton upon Trent, 1973. We're stood next to my dad's Ford Transit Diesel Mark I.

Me at eight years old, with my three brothers, next to the caravan I was born in.

Me and my brother Peter in 1976. At The Travellers Rest campsite in Hull.

Aged twenty-six, training to fight
an Italian heavyweight on Bartley
Gorman's land in Uttoxeter.

A promotional shot taken of me while
training, twenty-six years old.

Training with Bartley Gorman.

Me, Nobby the horse
and the caravan I lived in
on my land in 1992.

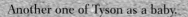

Me holding John Boy, aged two,
outside our first house. The Volvo,
which we'd sell, was ours.

Tyson, three months old.
Clenching his fist even then.

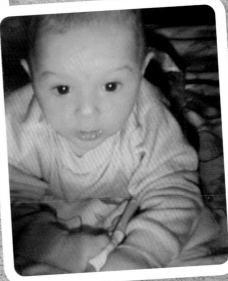

Another one of Tyson as a baby.

Me and Tyson, in 1989.
He would have been one year old.
Sat on my lap on Christmas day.

Shane aged four and Tyson aged
seven with my father.

My father on the left and three-year-
old Shane is in my arms, 1993.

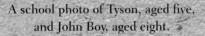

A school photo of Tyson, aged five,
and John Boy, aged eight.

Roman at two-years old.   Tommy, eight months old.

Roman on the left and Tommy on the right, in 2003.

John Boy at seventeen years old, showing my mother his new car. It's a family tradition to take pictures with new cars in my mother's driveway.

Left to right: My father sat down, my mother stood next to me, my uncle Henry Beenie sat down on the righ

not very good at sticking together; they're too busy fighting among themselves to get organized as a single voice to stand up for their rights as a minority. Part of being a Traveller is living your life from one day to the next. In 1995, the Traveller community began to have dialogue with the Irish government, discussing healthcare and education, and in 2000 a new law, the Equal Status Act, was introduced with the aim of stopping discrimination. In 2002, the Trespass Act was established to forbid Travellers from camping on traditional lands. In 2017, the Irish government finally gave recognition to Travellers as a distinct and separate ethnic group.

Because of our unhealthy suspicion of the British and Irish establishment, many of us don't consult a doctor as regularly as we should, and as a result our healthcare needs are not addressed; for example, there are more miscarriages than there need to be, and undetected illnesses that are discovered too late. The average Irish Traveller has a dramatically lower life expectancy of fifty-nine years, compared with the mixed national average of eighty-two years.

Discrimination toward Travellers is still alive and kicking. As recently as 2021, some Holiday Parks companies systematically discouraged us as customers, going so far as to circulate typical Gypsy surnames to the booking staff to look out for. The problem is that certain Gypsies and Travellers don't help themselves and create a bad name for the rest of us, because some of them do leave a mess behind for others to clean up, or fly-tip in rural places. To my mind these are not true Romani or Traveller, they are parasites of society. True Irish Travellers are respectable, well-dressed people and wouldn't dream of leaving a mess behind them. My mother was a true Gypsy, and she worked incredibly hard; she used to work in the fields, picking peas and fruit, she worked on farms and on the roads. In her day, they got on with settled people and had respect for their property. My father used to say, 'We need the settled people, they pay our bills. You respect them and they will respect you.'

I felt what I can only describe as
a big blue light flash across my eyes.
It took me a moment to focus, the
lights were dancing. I sucked in
a lungful of air, picked myself up off
the ropes, turned around and
got on with business.

6

Turning Pro

I first turned professional because I sorely needed the
money. I'd just come out of a spell in prison and times
were hard. I didn't have a vehicle, and so I was door-
knocking on foot, offering myself up for any painting and
pointing work in Halifax in Yorkshire. It's a bitterly cold
day early February, and I've been knocking on doors for
the last two hours – even if I want to, I can't stop, I've
got mouths to feed. Besides which, as my dad used to say,
'It's a numbers game, you knock on enough doors and
eventually somebody will want what you're selling.' And so
there I was, on my uppers, when the wheels of fate turned
mysteriously for the better. I ended up talking to a man
on his doorstep and striking up a good rapport with him.
'I don't have any materials of my own, sir,' I told him. 'I'm

down on my luck, but I'm a grafter and will work for you for almost nothing if you're prepared to get the materials and give me a chance.'

He looked at me squarely and said, 'I like you, so I tell you what, you come back tomorrow, and I'll have the materials here that you can work with. I don't know you but here's forty pounds in your hand now.'

I said, 'Sir,' since I called everybody *sir*, 'are you prepared to trust me with forty pounds?'

'I am, because forty pounds won't even scratch my wallet, but to you I know it's a big thing.'

What mattered even more to me was that he took me at my word and trusted me. The next day I went back, and he had all the materials for me, just as he said he would. Firstly, the ridge tiles with which I did the pointing on the roof. Next, I rubbed down his front door, under-coated it and painted it. I did the same for all his windows and window frames, upstairs and downstairs, all for the grand old total of £180. When he came to pay me, he pulled another two fifty-quid notes from his wallet and said, 'Good job, there's an extra hundred pounds for your effort.'

We shook hands and I was about to thank him for the work, when he said, 'How old are you, lad?'

'Twenty,' I said.

'What weight are you?'

'Eighteen stone.'

'Aye, you're a big lad and well put together, how tall?'

'Six foot three.'

'You should be a fighter. Follow me through to the back.'

He showed me pictures of Yorkshire fighting men as he scribbled something on a piece of paper. 'I'm going to give you a number to call. This person is a boxing promoter called Tommy Miller. You should call him.'

I did, that very afternoon.

'Mr Miller, my name is John Fury. A friend of yours has given me your number and he says you might be to help me out.'

'Help you out? What are you?'

'I'm a fighter,' I said.

'What have you done?' he enquired.

'Nothing.'

'Amateur fights?' he said, unimpressed.

'No, but I've been fighting all my life. Where is your gym? I'll come there and prove to you I *can* fight.'

The gym was in a big old broken-down mill in Burnley. I had on a pair of jeans, a T-shirt and a hobnailed pair of boots. I spotted him in the corner; he was in his early seventies with a pork-pie hat on. He looked like he had been through the wringer, his nose twisted and his eyes hooded at the corners. Indeed he had, as both an amateur and professional boxer, Miller had taken part in 250 competitions in his time as a fighter, later becoming a promoter and a manager. I wandered over, my hobnail shoes clacking loudly on the wood floor, the grain worn smooth by endless streams of sweat, blood and the odd tear. It stank of leather and perspiration in there. A fighter hitting a heavy bag looked at me briefly and returned to his training.

'Tommy Miller?' I asked, my head held high, my gaze steady.

'You're a big lad. So, you want to be a fighter? Well, you'd better realize that this is a funny game.'

'With respect, sir, I haven't got all day. Who do you want me to fight?'

'It doesn't work like that.'

'I've come all the way here from Halifax. Now can you get me a fight so I can make some money, or not?'

He looked at me and could tell I wouldn't take no for an answer. 'All right then,' he said, pointing to a bloke who was all of about twelve and a half stone, who was having his gloves laced up. I knew of him; he was a middleweight called Sean Layton from Chorley, a professional boxer with eight fights behind him. He stood at about six foot.

'Let's see how you get on with him,' said Tommy, his eyes lit up with a smile.

I borrowed some gloves and climbed in the ring. I was eighteen stone, and this guy was dancing around peppering me with a real mix of shots. He was much too quick for me, but I kept going, kept hunting him down and closing the ring down on him. Remember, I had done no ring work, I had no experience whatsoever; it was as if I had cement blocks tied to my feet, and this little wasp was buzzing around firing venomous barbs at me.

Finally, I said, 'Try me against a bigger fighter, this one's a bit tricky for me.' Tommy put me against someone closer to my size and I knocked him around a bit.

'Okay, okay, that's enough,' he said, his broken face lit by a smile. 'How did you learn to fight like that?'

'I've been fighting all my life.'

'I want you to spar with a lad from Leeds.'

It seemed I had jumped through my first hoop.

The fella who ran the gym in Leeds was called Peter Coleman. His son was an all-Ireland champion. The most arresting thing about the lad was the size of his head – it was as huge as a cannonball. And he had these sloping shoulders, as if he was a hod carrier by trade, and long arms and massively powerful legs. He was a little shorter than me, probably six foot one, and a light heavyweight. He was quite the opponent. 'Ah well,' I thought to myself, 'if today is my good hiding day, I may as well show them what I'm worth.' I wasn't scared; all I was there for was money to feed my son. What I lacked in experience and finesse, I hoped to make up for with a lot of heart and a burning desire to win.

I climbed through the ropes. 'Can I take my boots off, they slow me down a little bit?' I said to the owner, Peter. 'Have you got some pumps I can borrow?'

I put these pumps on, thinking that they might make me dance a little quicker on the canvas but, no sooner have we touched gloves, than he hits me almost spark out with a vicious uppercut. I spun around and went right over the rope. I felt what I can only describe as a big blue light flash across my eyes. It took me a moment to focus, the lights were dancing. I sucked in a lungful of air, picked myself up off the ropes, turned around and got on with business. I hunted him down, grabbed him in a clinch, leaned on him and walked him about a bit, throwing clusters of uppercuts and hooks to the side of his head, bish, bash, wallop. I didn't half give it to him!

We went three rounds together, after which Tommy Miller waved his arms and said, 'Enough, that's enough!' He smiled at me and tipped his pork-pie hat back a few inches on his forehead. 'You're a raw novice but you've got bigger balls than anybody I've ever seen in my life.'

I nodded, said nothing. I wondered if I had successfully passed through my next hoop.

'I'll tell you what,' he said. 'There's a boxing match in Halifax in five weeks' time. I can pay you five hundred quid and it's going to be televised. All I want you to do before you leave is sign a contract, I'll rush the paperwork through, and you'll need to get a full medical and a brain scan – which we will organize. In the meantime, I want you to go to the Brian Hughes gym in Collyhurst Moston in Manchester.'

'Right.'

Tommy seemed at a bit of a loss as to how I learnt to box. 'Are you sure you haven't boxed amateur before?'

'No,' I said, 'the only time I've ever put a pair of gloves on is when I was a lad mucking around with my dad.'

'Well, the thing is,' he explained, '*I'm* happy with you,

but the British Boxing Board of Control is going to need to see you before they can pass you fit for a licence. See, there's not many people who come straight into the professional fight game without any amateur experience, or any ring work. It does happen, but it's rare as hens' teeth.

'So, meet me Monday morning at Brian Hughes's gym and the board will be there to see you spar.'

I said that was okay but there was the issue of funds; I didn't have the money to keep going up and down to different gyms in the north. He advanced me £250, half my fee up front. And that was that.

Come Monday, I was at the Brian Hughes gym, as were Tommy and the board. They put me in with a boxer called John Joe Green, a veteran of about twenty fights and a current all-Ireland champ. Again, perhaps I should've been more afraid than I was, but as far as I was concerned, I knew I had a spirit in me. I knew I was a fighting man; what I didn't have behind me was a perfect record. In fact, I had no record whatsoever. Sometimes there are benefits to being the underdog, no one expects a great deal of you. So, in I climbed and boxed his head in – bing, bang, wallop!

The Boxing Board were sufficiently impressed and granted me my professional licence. I suppose it was a moment of minor triumph in my life, I felt like it was the beginning of a journey. And I was happy because now at least I could earn some money. The £500 fee was a fortune to me; it represented food on the table and the chance to buy an old motor to get around in my regular work. After that spell in jail, it felt like my life was taking an upward trajectory.

Shortly afterwards I was on *Fight Night*. I lost my debut fight against Adam Fogerty on points, but I gave him a good fight on national television. I went on to win my next seven fights. Strangely, the phone then stopped ringing and I was only getting approached for around one fight every six months. Apparently, managers wanted losers for their prospects to fight; safe-bet, tired journeymen that would make them look good. I was something of a dark horse – young, up-and-coming, hungry, and unwilling to be anyone's donkey. Boxing me was a risk to an established pro's unstained fight record.

Sadly, I had no one looking out for me in my corner. No manager nor fight promoter wished to support John Fury and grow his profile as a fighter. Why? Because I was a Gypsy.

In my short professional career of thirteen fights, I beat the Welsh and also the Italian champion on points over ten rounds, and in 1991 was ranked third in the country and fourth in Europe. But I wasn't getting the fights, with only thirteen bouts over eight years. I quickly became dispirited with 'the Fancy'. It's not only about talent. Making it as an international champion involves a cosmic set of conditions beyond your diet and fitness level; it's about having the right people and trainers around you and the time being right. Without somebody looking out for me, I managed to get to title level. Sometimes I idly speculate

how far I could've got if I'd enjoyed the benefits of sponsorship, and career guidance and support, and hadn't had
to do two jobs just to keep my family afloat financially. I
wasn't making any real money from Queensberry Rules
boxing; in thirteen fights as a pro over an eight-year period,
I made less than £4,000. Fighters often make excuses after
they've been beaten, but some of my challenges were
laughably one-sided. Like when I fought Neil Malpass. It
was my first ten-rounder, and at the time I had only had
a handful of fights and experienced six two-minute rounds,
while he had had over forty professional fights. I lost
narrowly on points.

From a financial perspective, the rewards for bare-
knuckle fighting were more tempting. It was never going
to be a full-time career, I promised myself, just a chance
to moonlight and make some extra cash alongside my
regular daily graft hawking. Looking back, Tommy Miller,
my professional boxing promoter, should have taken better
care of me. I had no one in my corner, no regular coach,
dietician, or physio; it was turn up, get paid. I'd had a long
time out of the ring, and no one was calling to set up a
fight with me. Then out of the blue Tommy called me on
a Wednesday to tell me I'd be boxing that Friday night.

'Yeah I'll fight,' I said casually. 'Who is it?'

'Henry Akinwande.' Akinwande was a future WBO title
holder.

Tommy must have thought to himself, *John Fury is a
good journeyman who'll put up a good show. He's got a big*

heart and he won't stop until he's knocked out. Yeah, he'll do.

So, for my penultimate fight as a pro, I faced Henry Akinwande, having had no training whatsoever. The sweetener was the offer of £900 for the fight, and as I needed the money I took it. I was doing well in the first two rounds, throwing some good body shots that shook him, but I had no conditioning (well, three days!), and I was soon tiring. Akinwande's hand-speed was impressive, and in the third round he dropped me with a big right hand.

The planets have to be in alignment to make a champion fighter; for me they never had a chance to start falling into place. I was too busy with my paternal responsibilities, trying to feed my kids.

When he heard about
the contract which had been
taken out on me, he got word
from his prison in York.

7

Dancing on the Cobbles & Life as an Enforcer

Three principles dictate the way I live my life: honesty, being true to my word and treating others with respect. When I look back on my life, I have for the most part achieved those values, it's only when others have riled me or darkened my family name that I've had to retaliate.

My mum was born in 1935 and grew up during the war years. Her father was from Redhill in Surrey; a hard man who had suffered the loss of two brothers to the Second World War. Crop and Ned Skeet were both bare-knuckle fighters of some repute; they fought to put food on the table for their families. Back then, as is the case today, bare-knuckle fights were illegal and had to be secretive underground events. In this sport, the fight goes on as long as it takes for one man to capitulate to the other, and they can take each other to hell and back before one of the fighters calls 'time'.

In 1867, the ninth Marquess of Queensberry sponsored the creation and introduction of a set of rules designed to protect boxers. This established the twenty-four-foot ring, the three-minute round with one minute's rest between each, the use of big gloves, the ten-second count . . . and that rather eccentric condition, that nobody wore springs in their shoes! The last *official* heavyweight bare-knuckle fight took place in 1889 and it lasted seventy-five rounds!

My mum's Uncle Crop was known to be the best fighter of his day; tough as a collier's boot, he had the strength of two men and could fight straight for an hour. Back then, gloveless fighters didn't make much money, so they had to fight regularly to make ends meet. As a result of these frequent brawls, they were very match fit and had good stamina, but the damage they sustained in the process was terrible. When my mother was a little girl, these Traveller gladiators looked so beaten about that they used to scare her; their forearms, which they used to block a hail of punches, had never been set correctly so they never healed properly, and were completely deformed, with bones protruding at unnatural angles beneath the skin. Back then, if you broke your arm you put a piece of wood on it and taped it up, then you just carried on with your work.

There are several things that distinguish boxing and bare-knuckle fighting from one another. First, the crowd;

bare-knuckle fighting attracts a more extreme crowd. There's a bloodlust, they want to see gore, to witness a man's jaw being smashed in front of them, bone on bone; to hear a man's cheekbone pop and watch him go down, his head banged repeatedly against a stone floor till it bursts like a watermelon. Whereas a boxing bout is heavily advertised and happens on a well-lit stage, a bare-knuckle fight is a secretive, underground affair, a place of shadowy faces spitting and shouting from the dark.

A boxer is first and foremost an athlete, and needs to be super fit to compete, even at an amateur level. There is a science to the sport, there's no two ways about it, and it's one of the most demanding sports there is. There are rules to the game, like not hitting your opponent on the back of the head, or punching below the belt, all of which are perfectly permissible in the world of its shadowy sibling.

Conventional boxing is much harder because the only weapons you can use are your fists, so you have to be a specialist of the craft, and the fitness required to be able to last twelve rounds for three minutes is staggering. Just as climbers attempting Everest must do so in gradual stages, acclimatizing themselves to the high-altitude thin oxygen, so too must any fledgling boxer. They work their way up from three-round fights, to eight rounds, and finally to twelve rounds; it doesn't happen immediately.

These underground fights don't demand anything like the same levels of fitness and finesse and are usually over within the first two minutes, because if a man my size is still there, he's going to require some urgent medical attention. My tactic was to get in there, throw a lot of punches, get the job done and get out as quick as possible. I was a big strong man with an iron will to win.

One of my first fights was in Riston, near Accrington in Lancashire. I was twenty-seven years old and easily outclassed the lad I was up against as I was still a professional boxer at the time, and was keeping myself fit in the long gaps between professional fights. The prize was a brand-new van which I won. Another one of my early bare-knuckle fights was in Preston, and guess what the prize was? A Sherpa van. Pretty soon, I had vans coming out of my ears, and almost enough of them to open a garage!

I was never beaten in a fight outside of the ring. In the ring you've only got use of a pair of gloves, but outside of it you've got everything: feet, elbows, head, teeth. And I used everything I had in these bare-knuckle fights. Also, I was prepared to fight anybody. Anywhere, any time. To get a stake in a fight you needed at least ten grand, so I sold my van, my lorry and my caravan to invest in myself.

To get fit for a fight I'd chop wood, and just like Ali did in Zaire in preparation for the Foreman fight, the 'Rumble in the Jungle'. I ran in army boots; sometimes I ran with a van tyre around my waist. I hit a heavy bag with bare fists to harden my knuckles. I didn't have a particularly hard punch, but I had spirit, guts, and an absence of fear. I also had something in my pocket which most bare-knuckle fighters lacked: experience in the professional game. Once you've learned the rudimentary skills of the fight game, how to throw a punch, how to feint, how to counter and anticipate, you're already well ahead in the stakes against a man on the cobbles.

One of the reasons I never lost was because most of my bare-knuckle opponents were second rate. They'd try to fight me square on, toe-to-toe, absorbing everything that I gave them. I was strong and they had no skill or ability; it was easy as taking candy from a child. Back then, compared to them I was very fit and, because I'd keep on at them without coming up for air until they were flat out on the floor, most of my fights were over very quickly. The year 1992 was a good one for me, when I faced an Irishman said to be the best bare-knuckle fighter of the time. With the stake I had in the fight, I made a sizeable amount of money. Unlike The Fancy (the pro boxing world), where I was often called up to fill in at the last minute, and for which I might get paid a paltry £500 for a professional fight, out on the cobbles I could make some *real* money.

Life as an enforcer

Someone with good mental health does not need to express themselves with violence. For about five years, between the age of thirty to thirty-five, I was an enforcer. I worked alone. Always. Maybe it was a deal gone sour, maybe somebody owed somebody else. People could call up and say they were getting bullied by somebody, or were in some kind of trouble, and for a fee I would go and sort it out in my own way. That took me into all kinds of weird and wonderful situations, and I met with some real oddballs. I was very matter-of-fact about it; either they stopped doing what they were doing, or in the case of somebody owing money – either they paid or they got a knuckle sandwich. I never used a knife, never used a gun. In all my years around violence, I never touched a blade. The only knife I possess is a penknife for opening the dogfood tins. My fists and head are the only weapons that I need.

There was a man, a gangland boss from the North, who had allegedly killed eight or nine people, but the police hadn't managed to prove it. I had an issue with him over a friend. One day I went to a garage to pick up a car and he was there, a big man about six feet tall, twenty stone, and a square head like Frankenstein's monster. With him were five of his heavies. I walked straight over and hit him with a right hand, and then put his head through a glass coffee table. Outside we got to it and had a full-on fight. In its dying moments, he was clearly beaten, and I heard deafening police sirens getting closer; suddenly there were bodies jumping all over us. Unsure of whether he was a plainclothes copper or one of the ganglord's henchmen, I slapped one across the face rather than knocking him out, just to be on the safe side.

A few days later a storm was building when two high-ranking plainclothes detectives came to the house and said they needed to talk to me about the ganglord I have served a good beating to. The taller of the policemen was about six foot five and introduced himself as a Special Detective. He asked me if they could have a word.

I've always been respectful to the police so I stood to one side, motioned for them to enter. 'Come in, say what you need to, then leave,' I said.

'I'm here to issue you an Osman warning.'

I'd received a few of them before. An Osman warning is issued by the police when they know there is a death threat or risk of murder directly attached to a person. 'The gangland boss has taken a hit out on you,' said the Detective. 'I understand you gave him a good hiding. If he dies in hospital, you understand that you'll be on a murder charge?'

'He won't die,' I said. 'Besides, he's big enough to fight and he's got a will to live, that man.'

'I admire your confidence,' the Special Detective replied ironically.

'I'm a fatalist,' I said. 'Whatever my destiny is, it's already written.'

Outside, it started pelting down with rain; it flew at the windows like knives. I was only in my mid-thirties but felt much older that day. *I'm getting too old to be looking over my shoulder*, I thought to myself.

'Thank you, gentlemen, I appreciate you letting me know.' I showed them out and waved as they drove off.

I heard nothing from the man who wanted me dead, or his goons for a few days. Nor did I hear from the Special

Detective. At the time, my brother Peter was behind bars. When he heard about the contract which had been taken out on me, he got word from his prison in York to the ganglord's people and calmed the whole situation.

Everything went quiet for a time, and I forgot about the Osman warning because I was more concerned about my father, who was very ill. Oddly, Peter, who had a thing for expensive cars and who was now out of jail, began to have dealings with the man who had wanted me dead, who sold luxury cars. My brother came round to the house one day and said, 'This man, John, he's terrified of you. He wants to put what happened between the two of you behind him.

'To be honest he's not such a bad guy, I've been around him for the last couple of months and he's actually quite an honourable fella. He has his reputation to keep intact, just as we have ours. He's frightened of what you still might do after hearing about him taking a contract out on you.'

'So what do you think we should do then?' I asked.

Peter thought for a moment, then said, 'Well, I'm thinking I could set up a meeting for next week, so you two can meet and shake hands.'

'Where?' I said.

'Somewhere public. We could pick a local shopping centre.'

The rest of the week went by very quickly, and the day came for me to go to this particular shopping centre. Obviously the police had got wind of it from a snitch, or heard on the grapevine that something was going down, and when I met the ganglord there was a heavy police presence; a helicopter circling in the air, and plainclothes coppers dotted around the shopping centre.

'How do you know they're plainclothes?' asked Peter, as we walked to the rendezvous.

'You forget I spent almost three years on the run,' I said. 'I can sense their presence at a hundred paces.'

'Well, they won't be needed because there's not going to be a problem . . . is there, John?'

'Not from me,' I said quietly.

As it happened, the man and I shook hands, and though I won't say we became bosom buddies, in time I too saw that he was a man of his word and could be trusted. A year or so later, he even came to my garage and bought a few old cars from me. I wish him no ill.

People have pulled a gun on me before and – given that I'm still here – it illustrates the point that most people are afraid to fire one. Which is a good thing. Only a few months ago I caught someone on my property who was trying to steal a classic motorbike of mine from out of my shed. At first I thought he was a builder, as there were a few on site, but then I saw him brazenly wandering out with my bike.

'I need this bike,' he said, reaching into his pocket and pulling out a pistol. I walked over and took the handle of the bike with one hand, and knocked him out with the other, then wheeled my bike back in the shed. I woke him up with a bucket of water in the face, kicked him up the arse and told him to get off my property.

Any man who carries a gun or a knife is a coward. They cause such trouble and pain and do such terminal damage. A member of our family was a victim of knife crime in August 2002. Rico Burton, my nephew, had been peacefully watching a boxing match on TV when he was stabbed to death. It was a waste of a good life; Rico was a fine lad and a promising boxer.

In the mid-1990s, the city of Manchester became a creative wellspring of house, dance, electronic and indie music, producing bands like The Stone Roses, The Inspiral Carpets and Happy Mondays, plus a raft of superstar dance DJs. This golden era of music in Manchester was known as 'Madchester' and at the centre of the scene was the Haçienda nightclub. Madchester's music was lubricated by MDMA, amphetamines and ecstasy. But beyond the fluffy scene of smiling emoji T-shirts, baggy trousers and floppy hats worn by kids out of their tree dancing until dawn, was a savage, seedy underbelly of dealers and lunatics with sawn-off shotguns. Madchester? More like the Wild West (or Wild North West).

For a brief time in his role as an enforcer, my orbit crossed paths with this world but, I might add, very much on the periphery. I had zero interest in trafficking drugs or partaking of them, that was against who I was. Besides, once a boxer, always a boxer – I kept myself fit and had a level of respect for my body. I was a one-man army for hire, and the drug dealers who operated across the city knew to leave me alone. I had a reputation, and they were aware that if they got on the wrong side of me and my Mr Hyde came out, the only way they could stop me was by popping a cap in my head. The police knew I wasn't directly involved in any drug enterprises. I was occasionally hired as a dial-a-nutcase, extra muscle who could be relied on to make sure things were done.

I realize now just how lucky I was to have come out of that time in one piece. Increasingly back then, I found myself looking at my children and wondering what the hell was I doing. I'd had enough of being an enforcer and felt that the longer I was in proximity to this world of nutters, the more the chance I'd lose my life and my kids would grow up without their dad. There's an old saying, 'If you live by the sword, you die by the sword'; that's to say, if you hang around trouble long enough, sooner or later you get burnt, as do those closest to you, the innocents. And I had no intention of my family getting in harm's way. I'll always be grateful to have escaped that time in one piece.

It might amuse you to hear that many years later, during my final spell in prison at Strangeways, I met Bez, the bug-eyed, tambourine-wielding, non-stop dancer from The Happy Mondays. I liked him and he certainly brightened the place up for the short time he was there.

I smelt death.

8

Wanderlust

For me life is all about making memories. It's not just about work. My take on work is you put your back into it, and take care and pride over your project. Whether you're laying Tarmac, building or training for a fight, it doesn't matter; it's the same rule for all: don't cut corners because it'll come back to bite you later on. In the mid-1980s, when I was in my early twenties, I was sat in a pub one day listening to a conversation that a couple of guys were having about how much work was to be had in Germany.

I thought to myself, *Germany is only a few hours away*. The next day my van was packed, and I was heading across the English Channel, bound for Rotterdam then on to Germany. I love history, and places like Berlin were fascinating to me as so much had gone on there.

Despite the fact that I couldn't speak a word of German, it didn't stop me finding Tarmacking and building work, which then spawned yet more jobs, as the quality of my work was very high. I slept in my van each night and showered at motorway services. My work took me to Heidelberg, Hamburg, Frankfurt; in fact all around. I was away for a couple of months at a time. Gradually, my understanding of the language improved a little, I bought myself a German caravan to sleep in and put together a team of decent guys who worked for me.

In Germany in the 1980s, come Friday afternoon everything stopped, and didn't resume till the following Monday. Unlike today, the weekend was properly considered a time of rest. After a long week of labour, I'd be exhausted and missing the family, which at the time consisted of John Boy, Tyson, and their mum, Amber. Every fortnight I'd fly back to Manchester and our home nearby, to see them for the weekend, and then it was back to grafting and sleeping in my German caravan.

Another place I remember driving through on my travels was Bosnia, which I visited shortly after the conflict there in the early 1990s. The signs of war were brutally obvious: buildings scarred by gunshot, houses reduced to rubble; in fact there wasn't a building that didn't have a bullet hole in it. I went to a restaurant and even the waiters had faces cut to pieces with fresh scars. It felt like a dead place and still looked like a war zone.

'How did you get here?' asked one.

'I came in my car. From England,' I said.

He looked at me with disbelief. I think his mouth fell open. 'And why you come?'

'I'm looking for work,' I answered.

'You English are crazy. There is no work here.'

It felt as if the ghosts of the newly dead were still among us and hadn't yet moved on after the atrocities they had suffered. As I drove across the pretty Bosnian countryside, I smelt death, and I spotted what I believed to have been recently used concentration camps, with barbed-wire walls and chimneys. By now I was close to the Bosnian–Croatian border. I was intrigued, but I thought, *the best thing I can do right now is get out of Dodge*. Looking back, my hunch was correct; exactly where I'd been driving were a number of Serbian death camps, where rapes, mutilation, starving and torture had been carried out as standard punishment.

Travelling is in my blood, and I'm never happier than when I'm moving through fresh pastures and landscapes, meeting decent folk and moving onto the next place. Among my favourite places is Canada, particularly British Columbia. I love Montreal as well, it's a beautiful city. I followed the road wherever it took me, generally preferring to avoid the cities and find work in the countryside – and what countryside it was! I remember being near Ontario, getting caught in bad weather. I pushed work as late as I could because there was so much of it to be had out there, and also because I didn't realize the snows came as early as late October. I'd bought a beautiful 1970 fastback Mustang, which to the uninitiated is a classic Mustang with a hard roof. It had a huge V-8 engine, with a deep throaty purr you could hear coming from a mile away. Anyway, the snows came and I was completely marooned, way out in the backwoods, and couldn't leave my cabin for a week.

It suited me being so far from anywhere civilized, surrounded by nothing but endless pine forests carpeted in waist-high snow. Before the snow arrived, I loved the colours of autumn foliage, the various shades of gold, purple and copper. Out in the backwoods, people were quite eccentric; I guess you become that way when you don't meet too many people. At night the bars, which looked like the saloons from old cowboy films, sometimes erupted into mass bar fights over some drunken comment.

I enjoyed the slow pace of life in British Columbia. It was a place where people found time to talk to strangers like me, interested to hear where you were from. No wonder it is consistently voted as one of the happiest places on planet earth to live – people treat each other as they should do, with trust, respect and being true to their word, the three pillars which I try to live by. I think if ever I'm going to leave the UK, I want to buy a place in British Columbia.

I got into classic cars over in that country – the Canadians are crazy for them. And they also knew how to fix them, however severe the problem might be. Dressed in overalls, with these gentle accents and giant hobo beards, they were like semi-domesticated Sasquatch. I was out in the back-woods on another occasion when a piston tore through the poor Mustang's engine. It was still light, and I began a long fifteen-mile walk through bear country to the nearest habitation, which turned out to be a farm. There were all these trucks in bits around the house, and more guard dogs than I have out in my yard today.

I knocked on the door. A tall lady opened it and asked me what I wanted. I told her I had a major problem with my car, and she called for her husband with a roar. He was a giant, stood about six foot five and had a beard wild as Poseidon's. 'What can I do for you?' he said in a gruff voice.

'I hear you know a bit about cars,' I said.

'Maybe. What seems to be the problem?'

I mentioned it was a 1970 Mustang and his eyes lit up with enthusiasm. 'Right,' he said, 'let's go take a look at her.' We jumped in his huge Ford Bronco, full of dogs, and off we drove, deep into the forest. On arriving, he opened up the bonnet and his head disappeared into the engine, emerging with a smile. 'Yup, we've got parts for this, no problem.' Next he pulled a length of rope out of his trunk and towed me all the way back to his farm.

That night he wouldn't have me sleep outside in the freezing cold in my car, insisting I slept the night under their roof in this big hut of a house they lived in. I was touched by his trust in me. He had not only gone out of his way to retrieve a perfect stranger's car, but also offered me shelter in his house. I ended up staying there a while as he gave me some work on his farm. My first job was to paint his grain storage towers, of which there were two and they were huge! That certainly kept me busy. I also did some asphalting for him, repairing his roof. It was a working farm; he and his wife and their son-in law worked themselves hard, and we would eat together in the evenings. At the table the farmer would often ask me about classic British cars. I stayed there for six weeks; just remembering their warmth and trust makes me smile. Maybe it was the authenticity of these folk in Canada that enchanted me. They were happy in their own skins; they didn't try to be anything they weren't. In my life I gravitate to people who are not trying to impress others.

My travels by van took me to other countries like Serbia, Hungary, Croatia and Romania. Sadly, the Mustang didn't come with me, and remained in Canada. What was I looking for? Was it just work, or was there something else, a restlessness within me?

Looking back, my favourite places were those that retained their old-world values, which seemed to be under attack in the corner of Cheshire where I'd built my house. The eighties in Britain was a decade of economic growth for many, encouraged by the Conservative government to spend, spend, spend. And so it became a time of excess, consumerism and materialism, where a new class of rags-to-riches types – who I generally referred to as 'jumped-up bums' – found themselves suddenly able to buy things on credit they had never had access to before. In that one generation, a lot of old values were lost, carried away on a turbulent current of greed and self-obsession. Values like never borrow, never have what you don't need, were the first to get washed away.

Even on normal days,
I was banged up for twenty-three
hours a day.

9

Faith

Faith is everything to me. As an Irish-born Catholic, the Lord was everywhere during my growing up. If you look around my house today, there are many religious artefacts, including a brass plaque of the Last Supper. My two dead brothers, Hughie and Jimmy, each have a crucifix on a chain draped upon their pictures. My father used to say, 'God puts you here for a reason. If it was all a big lie, Christianity wouldn't have lasted for centuries, or even millennia.' England is a Christian country and we were brought up to adhere to its moral code, and it saddens me that today we're encouraged not to talk about our individual faith, as if it's something dirty that might cause offence to other faiths. God said, 'You be ashamed of me, and I'll be ashamed of you.'

Every day I thank God for all the good things in my life
– my health and strength, my children and their
children, the food on my plate, and the freedom I enjoy
every day. At the end of the day, I'm happy for what I've
received out of life. I've had a full life. I've not got one
single complaint. So long as I have my health, I can't wish
for any more.

On both sides of my family, we were very religious.
Growing up, I remember Travellers' trailers had an altar at
the back, a sacred space where you could pray. We would
say grace each meal time, and say our prayers at night and
in the morning. God has never let me down.

When I went to prison for the first time, I never questioned my faith, nor tried to blame it on God that he had
landed me in such a horrible place; it was my actions and
my actions alone that had taken me there. It wasn't random,
it was supposed to happen, and I was supposed to learn
something from it. I know an old fella who works for me
and he's had four heart attacks, but he still comes to work.
'If I stop working,' he says, 'then it's all over. It keeps my
mind busy doing something useful. If I'm going to die, I'll
die on a ladder.' I know exactly what he means, he needs
a purpose. I take meals to local old folk who can't help
themselves; helping them makes me feel good and gives
me a purpose.

Jesus has come through for me that many times when
things have got rough. More times than I can remember.
When I was serving my final sentence in my mid-forties,

I felt like I was letting my family down because I couldn't be there with them. They never missed a visit and were there for me throughout the four-year stretch. Tyson would ring me most days and, on one occasion, two years into my sentence, he rang up sounding hollow and scared. He was in Sheffield hospital and his little son Prince, who was only one year old, was very ill with meningitis. 'They told me he's going to die, Dad.'

I said, 'Listen, son, they told me you were going to die, so that's rubbish.'

'How do you know, Dad?'

'I'm telling you now. I'm locked up in here and I can't get out, but what I can do is tell you that your son is going to be all right. Have you ever known me to be wrong, son? Think about it and tell me now. I'm going to call you tomorrow in the morning, and your son is going to be here. He's going to do a lot more in life.'

'Do you think so, Dad?' His voice sounded broken and small; he was desolate.

'I know so, son. Faith moves mountains. Now, stay strong, stay focused, stay positive, and let the professionals go to work and do what they were trained to do.' Just then the beeps went on the prison phone, alerting me to the fact that the money had run out. I slumped with despair; I could feel it pressing down like a heavy burden on my back. All my businesses had gone, everything I had worked so hard for had all gone. My children outside needed me, and I couldn't help them. It felt as if my life was falling apart. I couldn't eat a thing for thinking about Tyson and my little grandson.

The prison officer on duty was called Mr Fog. 'What's up, Fury?' he said.

'One of them days. Anyway, I won't be coming back out of my cell tonight; there's nothing wrong but I want to bar my door and gather my thoughts.'

'Why, have you had some bad news?'

'It's not bad news, my grandson is a bit poorly and my son is freaked out, that's all.'

He obviously saw through my attempt at nonchalance. 'Do you want to speak to somebody?' I assured him I didn't and that I was fine; meanwhile back in my cell, I sat down on my bunk and took up my old Bible. As I read, the words were leaping out at me in a more pronounced way than usual; it was as if the letters had been dipped in gold. The more I read, the calmer I was becoming. It isn't often you get feelings like that when you're in the midst of such a horrible situation; I knew my earliest possible release date was 2015 and we were only in 2011. Even on normal days, I was banged up for twenty-three hours a day, and this was a bank holiday. On bank holidays you're locked up from Friday afternoon till Tuesday morning, and only allowed out for your meals then it is back to your cell.

Twilight painted bars on my wall before evening fell. I was exhausted by the pressures of life, and my spirits were in a bad way again. Weighed down by them, I told myself, *You're never going to come out of this place. Something will happen to the family while you're in here.* The more I was overthinking, the worse my anxiety became. I said a prayer under my breath, 'Dear Lord, if this is my fate, if you think I deserve this in my life, then so thy will be done on Earth as it is in Heaven. But I'm in need of help today. Well, not me, my grandson. He's struggling a bit, but keep your hands on him and do the best you can for him, please.' Then I fell asleep.

My eyes open suddenly. I'm wide awake but I'm not in my cell, I am somewhere else. How can that be? I am completely compos mentis, my thinking is clear. Yet, at the bottom end of the bed stands the figure of a man and, though I can't see his face in much detail, I know it is the shape of Jesus. I look around me and it is as if I am in Aladdin's cave, it's piled knee-high with beautiful gold, sparkling diamonds and glowing emeralds; in fact, you could go to King Solomon's richest mine and it would be a poor substitute for where I am right now.

I blink my eyes repeatedly, open them wide and then close them again just to check I'm not dreaming. We've all had super-vivid dreams at some stage, but this feels very different, unlike any dream I've ever had, because every faculty seems honed and wide-awake, and the figure is *still* at the bottom of the bed. This has now gone on for what must be about thirty seconds, and then with a voice as clear as a bell, authoritative yet kind at the same time, the figure says, 'Everything will be okay.' And, as soon as I hear this, pure joy passes through me, like someone has just told me that I'm to be released from my prison sentence in the morning.

I blink, and when my eyes open, I am back in the graffitied walls of my small cell. I feel good, awesome. I have this sense of calm, the anxiety has completely vanished, the heaviness I'd felt. I put the kettle on and drink a cuppa tea. Then, happy as a leprechaun who's found a crock of gold, I start tap-dancing. It's four o'clock in the morning and I feel like bursting out into song! I'm so giddy with joy that I can't go back to sleep, nor can I wait for the prison officer to open the door at a quarter to seven in the morning, so I can rush to the phone and call Tyson to see how his boy is. Not that I need telling, I know that he's fine. Of course I do. I'll remember this date for the rest of my life, it's imprinted on my soul: 15 September 2011.

I dial his number, and Tyson picks up the phone. 'Everything's all right isn't it, son?' I ask and he says, 'Yes, Dad, it is. You were right again.'

I say, 'What happened?'

'He came right in the night.'

'What time was that?'

'He came perfect some time between three and four a.m.,' says Tyson. It was just before the time I had my experience. 'Son, you won't have any more problems with him; he might have a few ups and downs, but he'll be fine from now on.'

And you know what, after that moment, I pretty much sailed through the rest of my sentence – here and there I had moments when I was really struggling with being locked up and apart from my family – but from then on everything fell into place for me; I never struggled any more. My mindset completely changed. For instance, when my family came to see me and said, 'This is really hard work for you being in here,' instead of agreeing with them I'd say, 'Well it beats being dead, it may come close at times, but at least I can speak to people, and I'm getting a visit off you and that's something to smile about. This is my life now, and for the foreseeable future. You've got to stay strong and, remember, I'm always here for you at the end of the phone and I can still advise you, even from in here.'

I phoned them every day, sent them birthday cards, and never missed a single birthday. I did everything I could for them from inside, and in return they supported and stood by me and never missed a visit. They were my pillars, and I was still their rock. Something in me changed at around four a.m. on 15 September 2011. I began to look for the silver linings in every cloud.

Hope has given form to dreams and built empires. Hope is the small glimmer that grows in the darkness and eventually banishes it. Jesus said: 'Those who hope in the Lord will renew their strength. They will soar on wings like eagles; they will run and not grow weary, they will walk and not be faint.'

I pray to the Lord all the time. One prayer in particular I made while I was in jail, would have had massive repercussions on the rest of my life, had I not sought God's help. 'Dear God, don't let them send me to a prison miles away, keep me close by, so my kids can see me and I can see them.'

Two days after I made this prayer to God to keep me close to my kin, I had a visit from the prison governor himself. By now I had been at Strangeways for over a year. He said to me, 'You know what, Mr Fury, you're not a bad fellow. You should not be imprisoned. There was a fight you were involved in, and it got out of hand and went very wrong. But you have taken it like a man and you quietly get on with your work; you're always upbeat and keep your head down.

'As I'm sure you're only too aware, after a year, during which time we make a fair assessment of you, you should be sent away to a dispersal prison elsewhere.' A 'dispersal prison' has no short-timers in its population. The men in these places are Category A, the worst offenders and pure monsters: rapists, suicide bombers, child killers; the very scum of humanity, if such a word can be applied to them, as what remains of the 'human' in them is now largely absent. Among these types, in the interests of self-preservation you have to be on a constant vigil. The moment you relax is when some pyscho comes at you from behind and sinks a homemade shank into one of your vital organs.

But instead of sending you somewhere else, I'm going to keep you here, as over the last year you haven't

complained about anything – the food, the prison, or staff
. . . in fact, we could do with another fifteen hundred John
Furys here, to be honest.'

That was the best news I could possibly have. While
I'm not saying Strangeways was home from home, at least
it was Manchester air I got to breathe every day, knowing
that my family were under the same sky, just a few miles
away, experiencing the same weather. The have been impos-
sible for my family to travel to on a regular basis. Had I
not been allowed to remain at Strangeways Prison, I may
not have had the presence of mind to keep myself out of
trouble for four years behind an iron door. Why? Because
it was my family's weekly visits that kept me human, gave
me hope and something to look forward to.

I decided that if there was
a way out of this prison,
John Fury needed a lawyer.

10

Pride Before a Fall: Prison

In the Traveller community, temperatures can get raised very quickly; I've seen machetes appear and arms hacked off as arguments spiral into situations they never needed to. People are often seriously injured in the Traveller community due to extreme violence, and there are currently more Travellers in mainstream prisons serving life sentences than there ever have been. As a general rule, the only people Travellers hurt are other Travellers. Arguments usually start over trivial stuff, but then somebody enflames it by talking ill about someone else's family. The violence happens in a flash, and it's usually because somebody is defending the name and honour of their family. And it doesn't matter how big the person is who is throwing the insults, among Traveller folk it is a question of pride, and you throw yourself at them 100 per cent.

As I said, I've been incarcerated three times: the first two were when I was a young man in my teens; the final time, thirty years later, when I was in my mid-forties. During that long interim period I worked around the world, raised two families, and a lot of water calmly passed under the bridge; but I still had Mr Hyde living in the dark recesses of my head, patiently waiting for the day I really lost my temper so he could come out, causing carnage. That day finally came at a car auction, when I ended up in a fight with another Traveller, against whose family my own had held a grudge for a long time. It was an ugly fight, and what transpired was that the gentleman lost an eye in the process. And this is how I ended up in Strangeways, sentenced to an eleven-year stretch.

But this time I was a different beast entering those four walls of pain and sorrow, stupidity and hatred; I was no longer against the world, I just wanted to be back in it.

I'd come out of my cell for what the prison called 'Association time', and I'd look over the railings at these young lads squabbling with each other, working themselves up to one shanking the other in the gut over nothing. And I'd say, 'Boys, how long you got in here?' And they'd answer, 'Twelve months,' and 'Eighteen months, *mistah*.'

'You carry on talking about killing each other, and before you know it, one of you'll be dead and the other will end up doing twenty years. Me, I'm looking at indefinite public protection, I'm on remand and I probably won't see my family again. Let me give you some free words of advice, lads.'

Then they'd look at me and start listening, realizing this old boy was set for some very hard time. 'There is no point wasting your life in one of these hell holes. Think about what you could be doing on the outside. You could be eating fine food, having interesting conversations with good people, or spending time with your animals, but instead you're cooped up in here slowly rotting.

'You've got twelve months,' I said to one, 'and you've got eighteen months? That's just a shit-and-a-shake away from freedom. You can still get a decent job, find a nice girl, and have some self-respect back in your life again. The only one standing in your way is you.'

I thought on what I'd said to them; I had everything and more waiting for me on the outside. I was damned if I was going to rot in here for ever, I had too much to live for. I wanted another chance, if God would grant it, and in return I'd do anything to serve his purpose. I decided that if there was a way out of this prison, John Fury needed a lawyer. I'd had a few come to visit me in prison and my gut feeling was that they were just money magnets who couldn't have cared less whether I got thirty years or five, and who'd never visit my family to see that they were all right. *They're just chasing a pay check*, I thought to myself. *I've got two families out there depending on me and I've got to get out of here.*

Everyone in the nick is a barrister, at least they think they are, and everyone was doling out advice to me. I kept my own counsel. I decided that when it came to my trial I would stand in the court and tell the truth and nothing but the truth, every last bit of it. When the day came and I stood in the dock, I did exactly that; I tried to explain things as best as I could. 'Your Honour,' I said, 'I'm going to plead guilty to contributing towards an injury. But on the "intent" side, I'm not pleading guilty, because it was not my intention for him to lose an eye; it was a fight, it was human nature, and it's how I've been brought up. There's one thousand years of fighting man breeding in me, and I can't help that. I'm a family man, I love them, I love people, and I'm in here for the wrong reasons.

'Everybody deserves a chance in life, and I strongly believe that I don't deserve to be *lifed-off* with this horrible dirty sentence of "Indefinite Public Protection". I deserve time in prison, yes, but I don't deserve IPP, which is forever a stain on my character. Give me twenty-five years but please at least give me the prospect of one day being free. Please try and see fit to show me a little mercy.' The judge had a long po-face. He adjourned for a day report, which was bad news – it looked like I'd be getting life.

The barrister who'd said very little so far finally piped up. 'Your Honour, I've listened to what my client has to say and there is some truth in it. He's never been in trouble in twenty-eight years, he's got a big family and a business on the outside, and his son has a very good chance of becoming the world heavyweight champion. These things matter among the Travelling community. In the past, John Fury has only ever visited violence on other Travellers, never wider society, therefore he doesn't qualify as being a danger to the public. Now a danger he most certainly was to fellow Traveller Mr Sykes, but to the wider world he is no threat.'

My eyes flicked to the man with my life in his hands. He looked like Satan with a wig on. He was fiddling distractedly with a pen. I stood ramrod straight, like my grandfather, to receive my sentence. In my mind I said, *Lord, if you can help me, now is the time. Your will be done, this is my fate, this is my life and I accept it.*

Horsehair Satan cleared his throat and addressed the court with a voice that could have created ice cubes: 'I've listened to what you said with some considerable interest and it has swayed me. You are clearly a very intelligent man and I'm going to give you a determinate prison sentence.'

Thank you, Lord.

'Thank you, sir,' I said, knowing that if I got twelve years for good behaviour, I could be free in six and would still see the green grass of home.

'You'll go to prison for twelve years, and because you've been truthful, I'll give you ten per cent back, so now you'll serve a term of eleven years.'

As they led me down, I sang, the 'Green Green Grass of Home'.

Looking back, I have no criticism of the prison staff. When I first arrived, one of them gave me a heads-up. 'We know a bit about you, Mr Fury, and we know what you're capable of. What you have to understand is that in here we are the boss. You've got quite a bit of time to do, and as long as you remember that this is our domain, you'll be all right. You've got two options, you can make it hell for yourself, or you can treat us with respect and receive respect back.'

I waited till he had finished and then I said, 'You won't get any trouble out of me, sir. I'm not anti-establishment and I'm not anti-authority. But what I am going to do is look after myself.'

'You can do that, but be sensible, and just remember what you're in here for. Trouble will present itself to you while you're inside, it's up to you how you choose to deal with it.'

I nodded and said, 'I want you to know that I have the greatest respect for you and your colleagues, but if somebody comes into my room and tries to take my things, I will respond. Will I come to you if I have a problem? No. Will I mither you for anything? No. Will I do as I'm told? Yes, I will. I will not look for trouble in any shape or form, but if trouble comes to me and I've got to have it, I will have it, because I have to defend myself. My family outside needs me like roses need the rain, and I will do whatever I can to make sure I cause you the minimum of fuss so I can get back to them as soon as possible.'

I wanted the next five years to be productive, and I undertook to learn as much as I could, and absorb anything they were teaching that was going free. That included welding, plumbing, kitchen-fitting, plastering, bricklaying and painting and decorating. The courses lasted sixteen weeks apiece, and so time began to pass as my skillset increased. I also learned my way around the dark arts of using a laptop. Believe me, for an anti-tech person this was a considerable leap! The only machinery I trust is beneath a car bonnet, and that's just the old ones, not these modern ones that are controlled by computers.

I began to read a bit, and the book that stands out during my time in there was *1984* by George Orwell. I also read Jeffrey Archer's trilogy on his time in prison, and fair dos to the author, he did his time and took what he owed to society like a man. But I also read Jack Johnson's story; he was a Black boxer who was such a force of nature, even during a time when Black people were segregated and treated like less than human. He was the champion heavy-weight of the world at the height of American racism, and he dangerously flew in the face of controversy when he married a white woman, which was then against the law.

But most of all I read the Bible; it kept me focused and thankful, and shone a light on the right path so I could find my way through the darkness. Prison can be a mine-field for the individual who doesn't want to become institutionalized by its routine, or accrue extra years inside for fighting and becoming a problem within the system; you can keep your head down, with the best intention of trying to avoid conflict, but you can't control the actions of others towards you, and sometimes trouble just lands on your lap, uninvited. Over the course of my spell at Strangeways Prison, there was only one occasion when I had to physically assert myself and, not surprisingly, this happened in the first week of my eleven-year sentence.

There was a small gym attached to my wing, comprised of a couple of running treadmills and some free weights. One morning, I'm using the facility when this enormous Middle Eastern looking roid-head comes walking over. He's a lifer, a bodybuilder with huge thighs and arms like tree-trunks and, by the way he holds himself, anyone would think he was King of Persia. He tells me he wants to run on my treadmill. 'There's another one over there,' I say with a friendly tone.

'No, I want this one,' he says flatly.

I'm not looking for trouble, I want to get out of here and see my family again, and I will do my best to keep my nose clean, but there are certain unofficial laws in prison that you need to observe. One is, no matter how small you may be and no matter how big your challenger is, unless you want to be treated like a bitch for the rest of your time, you must put up a fight if the fight comes to you. Especially in the first week or so.

My mind does some pretty rapid arithmetic as I look first at the layout of the room, the position of the CCTV cameras and then at his body. Muscle does not maketh the man; this huge beast may be pumped till the veins poke out of him, but – unlike me – he's spent much of his time in the dark and has been living off prison food for the past several years. I however, up until recently, have had plenty of sunshine as a free man, and have eaten well with lots of vegetables and nutritional goodness. My belly accounts for that and that's a good thing, because when this bloke looks at me he doesn't see much of a challenge – just a fat guy who's in his forties and out of shape.

I make to walk off as if I've deferred to him, and then I swing round, hit him clean on the temple and he goes down like a big lump. Just out of camera range he lies on the ground. For a moment I'm worried I might have killed him. I slap his face a bit and he groans as he begins to come to. 'Come on, come on wake up, you big Jessie. You're not dead, you've just been knocked out, that's all.' I'm not angry, not at all; besides, he isn't worth it. It took one shot to fell this inflated Minotaur and now, before one of the screws begins wondering where two big men have disappeared to, I need him up on his feet again and out of here so I can resume my run on the treadmill.

When I shortly bring him round I say, 'You've learnt something today, big fella. Never tangle with a guy who has fought for a living and eats free-range eggs – you'll never win.'

He looks at me, confused. 'And one more thing,' I continue. 'Next time you pick on someone smaller than you, think twice about it, as John Fury will be watching you, and next time I may hurt you for real.'

He looked at me with flat, submissive eyes, the swagger now gone as he left the gym slump-shouldered, disgraced and pathetic. After I humbled him that morning, he was never again the same bully, and though silent on the matter, I believe the prison officers were aware of the favour I'd unintentionally done them. I know they'd been intimidated by him, and he was never out of line with them again.

People are for the most part pack animals, none more so than in prison where they follow and kowtow to the strongest or meanest specimen. I wasn't looking for followers in there, nor was I looking for friends, and I made that point emphatically; in the canteen I ate alone, outside I walked around the yard on my own, just as I exercised solo. When somebody looked at me for half a second longer than they should've done, I locked eyes with them until they dropped their head and walked away. I had established my sovereign territory and right for respect with my treatment of the Minotaur gentleman, now all I wanted was to be left alone to do my time and come to terms with my crime.

There was one more attempt to rouse me into violence and clock up extra time. Towards the end of my sentence, in order to ready me for my reintegration back into society, I was afforded a level of freedom at an open prison. I had no reason to complain, I had a job on the outside which involved leaving at six thirty in the morning on a bicycle and returning at seven thirty at night. I was allowed home visits, plus my regular timed visits with the family; everything was going well. I'd repaid the judge's trust in me by not putting a foot wrong all the time I was in prison.

My potential nemesis appeared in the form of a sly and twisted gangster. He was coming to the end of a thirteen-year stretch for murder and decided I was his next target. It was 2013, and Tyson's dream to be the heavyweight champion of the world was only four fights away from fruition. I wanted so much to be there for him, it had been purgatory only being able to watch his fights after the event on TV, rather than be there in his corner.

His last fight had been against two-time cruiserweight world champion, Steve Cunningham, and Tyson had been baiting him while leaving his guard open, and in the second round Cunningham clubbed him with an overhead right that floored him. Of course, as we were to see a few years later against Deontay Wilder, the only thing that will keep my Tyson lying down on the canvas is if he's been Superglued to it or he's dead. Tyson had bounced back and knocked Cunningham out in the seventh round. The dream of being the undisputed champ, a dream he had nurtured and worked so hard for all of his life, really felt like it was going to happen. My brother Peter had trained him while I was in prison, and it was vital for me to help Tyson on the last leg of his journey to the throne.

A voice beyond my cell door, in the corridor, said, 'That's how good that gypo son of yours is. He's not worth a fucking shilling if a little thirteen-stone man can knock him down.' I felt the switch flick in my head as my body filled with adrenaline, and blood started thundering in my temples. *Calm, check, breathe, check,* I told myself, but I couldn't stop the rising red mist. And still the man kept on, 'He's a worthless gypo just like his father.'

Locked in my cell, there was that much rage inside me I began repeatedly butting my head against the steel door. Fortunately for gangsta man, I wasn't going anywhere while the door was locked, for the moment I was stuck. So the burning steam of Mr Hyde began to recede, the bubbling blood stilled and I started to breathe regularly once more.

Revenge, I told myself, *will be best served cold on this occasion. I wondered, What will really hurt him? This man is a coward, he's used to getting into people's heads and undermining them with mental cruelty. And because he is serving time for murder, and because of his reputation as a gangster on the outside, even the prison officers are cautious of offending him lest they receive a visit at home one night – or, worse still, when they're working, and their wife or kids are visited.*

Just as vampires survive on the blood of others, gangsters thrive on fear. That fear creates reputation, and reputation is how they hold power over their miniature kingdoms. They are usually physically useless and couldn't punch a hole in a paper bag if their life depended on it; instead they rely on the muscle of a few knuckleheads to do their dirty work. A gangster's skill is working out others' weaknesses – including his own henchmen – and using those against them. But in order to retain their status, they have to occasionally prove themselves worthy of their lackies' loyalty and attempt to prey upon larger or more dangerous specimens like me. Otherwise the top dog looks like he's gone soft, and even one of his generals with half a brain may choose to challenge him. That's how the animal kingdom works and, dare I say it, the human world too, whether you're a banker or a gangster.

He picked on the wrong person the day he chose to try and get into John Fury's mind and start twisting his pathetic little knife around. And while Mr Hyde had come out and red mist had started to fill my cell, he had now gone; as evening wore on, there was just a sense of calm as I plotted retribution for his comments about my son. *I'm going to humiliate him in front of the entire prison population*, I thought. *It will be outside in the exercise yard, so they can all see him for the physical runt and mental bully that he is.*

The next day I get my opportunity. I spot him outside, holding court in the yard, doing his swaggering gangsta walk as if he has a pebble in each of his shoes. A few feet away from him are his pit bulls, looking about as dangerous as pantomime dames.

'Hey!' I say, 'I want a word with you for what you said about my son last night.' I'm getting closer and I see his bodyguards twitch into action. Stage one: they're throwing me the look. I keep talking, 'Now, at nearly fifty years old, I'm nowhere near as good as my son, but even with a broken back I could still beat you.' I rip my shirt off and throw it to the ground. Stage two: the pit bulls stand up and spread their shoulders out.

The shrill of conversation and laughter in the exercise yard dies to a murmur as all eyes are focused on the present unfolding drama. Unholy place that it is, it is quiet as a church, and this retribution is somewhat biblical. As he turns around to face me, my nemesis seems to visibly shrink. His dogs don't put up a fight or try to build a wall around him. Sometimes even morons sharing a brain cell know when not to engage a person with a calm measured storm brewing inside him. They part to let me through and move to a safe distance.

The weasel pulls out his mobile phone and holds it out to me as if it's an olive branch. 'Do you want to use my phone, *mate*? Call anyone you like,' he stammers.

I grab it from his hand and, like a Victorian teacher punishing a badly behaved pupil, swat him hard around the ear with it. 'Right,' I say, 'let's see what you're really made of. Get behind the wall now, and I mean now!'

He starts to scuttle. 'Fucking *run!*' I shout.

The screws see everything but are letting it happen. They know their life will be easier and safer once gangsta boy is removed from power. I get on with them; after all, it's not their fault I am in jail, it's mine. I have good conversations with some of them and will even share a game of pool – to the disgust and against the advice of other inmates who say, 'Don't talk to them.'

'Why not, you idiot? They're just people doing a job,' I'd say.

The prison governor was a decent individual. When the Traveller who had me banged up found out that I was now in an open prison, he complained to the prison authorities. In response, they demanded that I be sent back to Strangeways Prison on the next available bus. The open-prison governor was a man of principle, and did his best to stick up for me. 'Are we not in the business of rehabilitating people here?' he responded. 'John Fury has earned his right to be in my open prison, he's done a lot of time behind the door. And besides, there is not a single blemish on his record since he's been within our walls.

'And, I spoke with Strangeways this morning, and they loved him too. All I can say is I wish there were more like him here. I'm the governor of this nick and John Fury's staying. End of.'

I said to him, 'Thank you for sticking up for me like that, no one has ever done that for me before.'

'We gave you a test and you passed with flying colours, Mr Fury,' he replied.

Looking back on that last stretch inside I was a very different individual to the previous younger John Furys who'd been locked up. They wanted to fight everything in front of them, barring the staff. But by this time in my life, I had learnt to look for the opportunities in even the darkest places, and that old saying, 'Every cloud has a silver lining' I believed to be absolutely true. Instead of losing myself to a deep depression, giving vent to my rage and feeling sorry for myself, I had found a kind of peace by helping others manage their thinking and depression. I took no heed of dickheads, parked my ego, got on with my sentence and stuck to the credo of do as you're told and keep your nose clean.

I loved helping other people in jail. I remember one young prisoner who was very down. I asked him what the matter was and he told me in less elegant terms that he suspected his wife was having an affair.

'Why?' I asked.

'Because she didn't turn up for my visit.'

'Prison is not like the outside,' I told him. 'We've too much time and we end up clock-watching. Everything becomes magnified in here and your mind twists things, creating ugly scenarios and thoughts about people that are just not real. But out there,' I said, looking up at the barred window, 'people have busy lives with doctors' appointments, jobs, kids to manage, illnesses, commitments and a million things to do. Sometimes unexpected things turn up that need dealing with.

'If your wife loves you, then there will be a very good reason that she didn't pick up the phone and tell you she couldn't make her visit . . . Call her and listen to the reasons first, don't blow your top and don't judge her for something she may well not have done. Now, if it is the case that she *is* seeing someone else, then she's not worth keeping anyway, and she's done you a favour. But think before you act, because if you let it get to you, you'll end up doing something stupid in here and adding unnecessary time to your sentence.'

Later, before lock-up at eight thirty p.m., he knocked on my cell door and stuck his head in. 'John,' he nodded, 'just wanted to say thanks and you were right. Spoke to me wife on the phone and reason she didn't come today was cos she had an emergency – our son had a heart murmur, she rushed him to hospital.'

'Sorry to hear that, how is he?'

He nodded. 'He's okay, ta.'

'Well done, lad. Just remember in future, before you let anger take over, learn the full story. Prison is like an acid test for your true friends and loves, it has a way of weeding out the crap in your life, and people who don't care about you. Your wife clearly does care about you.'

During the two-hour visits from them when I was inside, I'd try and gain as much understanding of what my family had been up to over the last month, but then as soon as they'd gone, I too would turn things over in my head for days and nights afterwards, always wondering, *Is something going on that I don't know about? What are they not telling me?* I tried to remember the advice I dished out to others, namely that, 'Everything becomes magnified in prison and your mind twists things.' I suppose it was that old family paranoia that ran in my genes.

When I finally came out of prison as a forty-nine-year-old man, that first week back in society was very difficult. I felt like going back to my cell and locking myself in. I didn't feel like a father, I had a distinct sense of disconnection because I'd been on my own for so long. I now felt numb, dirty, horrible and useless, like a waste of space. I believed my family were secretly embarrassed about me.

I had become semi-institutionalized and too used to my own company. I'd shared a cell with myself as no one was prepared to sleep in the same room as me, for fear of what I might do to them. I had trained on my own, eaten on my own, walked on my own; I had become unsocialized and uncomfortable around others. I had no friends in prison. So when I was released, I felt very much on the outside.

Under my brother Peter's watch, Tyson had kept a clear unbeaten record. My son now had an upcoming world title fight against Wladimir Klitschko. I couldn't argue with that, Peter had done a fine job, just as my brother Hughie had before him, until he sadly passed while I was in jail. But each time I went to Peter's gym, I felt as if I was making a nuisance of myself, like a spare part. I really felt like going back to prison. Had I become like Brooks, that old man in *The Shawshank Redemption* with the pet crow, who is lost on the outside, fails to make the adjustment and hangs himself?

I'd had only eight months remaining of my sentence when my brother Hughie passed away. Hughie was ill in a coma in Lancaster hospital, but he had been in a coma before and pulled through, so I assumed the same would happen this time. One evening, as we cons were all in our cells, I could hear keys rattling in the distance. They were a long way away, but I knew just where they were headed. *He's coming to me.*

There are 1,499 other cells here that he can go to rattling his keys, but this visit is for me, I just know it.

The keys are going jingle, jingle. Then I hear him climbing up the steps to the second floor and walking closer, the floor clanking beneath his boots. All of a sudden he does the infamous stop and turn around, so he is facing my door, and now he's putting the key in the lock. It all seemed as if it was in slow motion.

'The governor wants to see you, Mr Fury.'

In the warden's office I sat down and said to him, 'I know it's bad news.'

'I'm afraid so, Mr Fury. I have to tell you that your brother sadly passed away a little earlier today at about six o'clock. I'm very sorry for your loss,' he said with a slight consolatory nod.

It felt like a fuse had blown my mind, everything turned black. 'Thank you very much for telling me, sir,' I said. As I walked back down the corridors to my cell with the prison officer, it felt like it was the longest walk I had ever taken. Never mind the green mile, this was the dark mile. When we lose someone we love, I believe a part of us dies and is lost for ever. When he shut that door and turned the lock, I felt as if I couldn't care less if it ever opened again. I was forty-nine and I'd spent the last four years banged up. I'd tried my best to rehabilitate myself, and now I had this to deal with. I shut the world out even more. Other cons came up to me, offering their condolences, and I thanked them, putting on my tough guy face, but inside I was dying.

The prison warden was very considerate regarding my attending the funeral. 'What we're going to do is allow you to attend your brother's service on your own. Usually we send someone with you, but I believe you can be fully trusted. We'll let you out at nine thirty in the morning, so treat it as if it was a day's work and be back here for four o'clock.'

'On second thoughts,' he continued, 'be back before seven thirty.'

A few days later, I was present at Hughie's funeral. I watched his coffin being lowered into the icy ground. It was cold enough to see your breath in front of you. Then I kissed my mother goodbye, told her I'd see her when I got out, and quietly left before the end of the service, catching a bus back to prison. Heartbroken by Hughie's passing, I was back in my cell by four p.m.

Coming out of prison was definitely harder than going in. The night before I rejoined society, I couldn't sleep a wink. The next day, outside the prison gates and feeling the breeze on my face for the first time was wonderful, but it was also unnerving, scary, exciting and joyful all rolled into one. Just before I left the prison, I was given my personal belongings and clothes in a bag, as well as a sackful of letters I'd received during my time here. I ditched the clothes and kept the letters. As I was waiting to leave, I noticed I was shaking from head to foot, as if I had the rigors from a chill. Chantal, my girlfriend, picked me up and, as we drove home, I was fighting to control my breathing and my heart was racing nineteen to the dozen. For those who have never experienced a panic attack, the anxiety is so acute it affects your breathing and the ability to think clearly; you really think you're going to die.

Chantal said, 'Why are you breathing like that?'

'I'm having a panic attack,' I told her.

'But why are you panicking? You've left prison.'

That was not the end of it. To celebrate my coming out of jail, Peter had booked a restaurant at the Trafford Centre and the whole clan would be present – Tyson, my other boys, the whole family. The prospect of it scared the hell out of me. All I wanted was to be left on my own. I felt completely lost. Back at Chantal's, I switched on an old black-and-white film to distract myself. I was watching it but I wasn't watching it, I was there but I was not there. I felt completely remote and distant from humanity, as if I was on Mars. It was the strangest feeling. I drank four pints of water one after the other. My hand was shaking terribly, and I wondered if I had developed Parkinson's disease from too many knuckles to the temple over the years, or maybe motor neurone disease, which is something that my father suffered from.

This paranoia and anxiety carried on for days; it felt like an out-of-body experience. One day, I had to go and meet the parole board, and I was so paranoid I might say the wrong thing and they would put me back in prison again. At the probation meeting they asked me what I was doing for work and my mind went blank.

Something, you idiot!

The best that I could come up with was, 'I'm washing cars.'

But I wasn't washing cars. I owned a garage and I was selling bloody cars. The meetings usually lasted thirty minutes, but in my fragile state it felt like they lasted hours. Every time I walked to the door of their office over the next four years, I felt as if there would be a comedic policeman waiting for me on the other side of the door. 'Surprise, surprise, you're going back inside, Fury!'

I was living in a horror story inside my own head. I didn't feel like I could talk to anybody about this anxiety and, because I wasn't sharing it, it began to grow in my head like a snake. I remember Chantal saying to me one day, 'You're not the same man that went to jail, you're someone else, John.'

I went back to my farm, and just being with the horses and my grandchildren made me feel better.

One of my boys gave me an old seventies Gypsy trailer which I slept in for days, rather than the house which felt too much like my prison cell. It was to be a solid year before I began to return to my former self and feel a sense of belonging again. That's the price you pay for doing time in prison.

It was vital that my older boys knew just how much I still loved them, despite the arrival of their first half-brother.

11

Fatherhood

Unlike my upbringing, which was challenging when it came to school, I wanted my boys to have a stable start to their education, one in which they could stay at the same school for the first ten years of their life. Because of my family's itinerant lifestyle, I'd never managed to settle in one class long enough for any teacher to coax me out of the shell into which I'd retreated, and develop me; we'd already be on the move to our next place. But for Tyson it was a whole different story.

I had bought and rebuilt a house in Styal at the age of twenty-six; the kids went to a small primary school nearby that had no more than thirty-five pupils. Tyson really blossomed here and fitted in brilliantly; he was accepted by the class, really liked by his teachers, and was near the top of the class in many of his subjects. And while he may not have been the most confident kid and was prone to anxiety, he had plenty of friends and was a happy boy. As a father you want for your kids what you never had. I'm grateful that I was able to give my boys a strong start to life, and then an environment they could work in. I started up a very successful second-hand car garage in the front yard of the house; Tyson would wash, shine and park all manner of cars from Porsches to Ferraris, and that's probably where his enduring appreciation of beautiful sports cars comes from.

As a young man I was very different to look at than I am today, with tar-black curly hair, a bubbly personality, and a twinkle in my eye. I always seemed to draw women to me. I had Porsches and Rolls-Royces in the driveway and dripped with gold jewellery. Some said I was the spit of a young Richard Burton, I certainly had his interest in the fairer sex. But a change was waiting for me a little further down the line; one which was less interested in all the shallow bubbles of wealth.

My first wife Amber and I had a rocky patch and, following one particularly ugly argument, she went to live with her parents to give us both some space. She stayed away for six months, and in her absence I began seeing Chantal, who in time was to become my son Tommy's mum. The relationship blossomed and deepened; in fact I'm still with this fine woman today all these years on. Chantal became pregnant early in our relationship and it was with a lump in my throat that I made my confession to Amber and told all my sons from my first marriage that they had a new half-brother on the way. It wasn't an easy pill to swallow but, for the most part over the years, they've been very accepting of my two sons from this new family, Roman and Tommy.

It was vital that my older boys knew just how much I still loved them, despite the arrival of their first half-brother, and I told them, 'I will never leave you. I will never forsake you. I will clothe you, feed you, drive you where you need to be, and be here for you until I take my last breath.'

And to Chantal I said, 'I'm one of the most stand-up people you'll ever meet. My name is John Fury and those children are my life. They come before any lady or anybody. I'll be right here for you and take care of you. But if ever you come between my boys and me, I'll walk away and I'll never come back.

'If my sons need me, I will have to drop everything to be there for them too. Half of me will always be with the family. If you'd rather this finished so you can meet someone who can be with you *all* the time, I fully understand that.'

Even though my sons still looked up to me as the head of the family and their dad, I knew the pain I was causing them. I was twenty-nine years old, ten years Chantal's senior, and my obligation was to keep those boys of mine on track so they could have a good life. One day, in late 1994, I made a promise to myself that my life would no longer be about me, it would be about my children. I shuttled between the two households, one in Styal, the other in Salford, making sure my kids wanted for nothing. All my time was dedicated to them.

Chantal's father was quick to notice the change in me and told me, 'You've been through hell what with your having to take care of two families, but you've never failed them. And I notice that where you once dressed in a snappy suit and sat behind the wheel of a Porsche as if you were en route to a movie set, you're now happy with driving old cars, a cuppa tea and a cheese sandwich. I salute you.'

Not everybody did, however. Many people ostracized me for having two families; they couldn't understand how I worked. My own father said to me, 'Son, why have you created such a load to carry on your shoulders? No man can bear all that.'

I said, 'I can bear it, Dad, and you know why? Because I love every one of them.'

When I die, I'd like them to put the epitaph: 'John Fury, a man of extremes' on my gravestone. I may be a fighter but the best of me is as a father.

I draw strength from my family and willingly give it everything. I did my best shuttling between both homes and tried to keep everybody happy. These days I lead a simple life. When I'm not helping Tyson or training Tommy, I still spend my time going between my kids' houses.

My lads

My eldest son is called John Boy. He's sensible and has a good head on him. When I was away in prison, he was still a young father and had quite a few kids. But in my absence he had to look after everybody and everything. He became the man of the house in my place. I knew the lifestyle I was leading meant that somebody would need to step into my shoes if anything happened to me.

He seemed to blossom when he was given an opportunity to grow as a man. He's always been independent, and he's never asked me for any money. He does his own thing and he's a jack of all trades, whether it's buying and selling cars, or making a profit on scrap metal. When I asked him what he wanted to do with his life recently, he said, 'Dad, I only want to live in the world not own it. I'm living in the world with my family and it's never going to get any better than this.'

I owe much of my business success in life to my eldest son. I wasn't in the habit of hiring staff, as most people found me too intimidating. I'm also a stickler for punctuality and always turn up quarter of an hour early wherever I go. If somebody rolled up five minutes late, that was disrespectful to me and I'd sack them immediately. John Boy is a grafter and we work well together.

Tyson is a one-off. What he does to inspire people who experience mental health issues, and his continual fight with his own demons are nothing short of inspirational.

As a person he's a fine human being and a wonderful father. As a boxer he is blessed with skills even I can't explain.

Shane is the next oldest after Tyson. Like his brother John Boy, he was always a listener and a watcher; he didn't say much but he took it all in. When it comes to business, Shane is a landscape gardener and also a builder. He lives close to me, he's a real grafter and works six days a week. But he's also a solid family-oriented guy with good values. He stands at six foot six and weighs twenty-five stone. He's a big man. Who knows where the height of my boys comes from. Until they grew up, I was the tallest in the family. My mother's father was five feet eleven (which was considered tall in the 1930s) but that's as big as they got.

Shane was aggressive and big for his years, even as a young lad. He would walk through a wall rather than around it. I remember getting a telephone call from a colleague, 'Shane is with his cousin Rico and they are fighting thirty men from the McGinley family outside the Trafford Centre.' By the time I arrived, the fight was over and they'd been arrested. Shane was matter-of-fact, as usual.

He was also a little accident-prone as a kid, though not always entirely through his own making. I remember as a young boy he nearly lost an eye, when Tyson was playing with a bill-hook. He must have spun around and accidentally caught Shane with it. I got a phone call and when I arrived, I could see the bill-hook had cut him badly in the corner of his eye. Yet another express visit to Wythenshawe hospital. The doctor informed us Shane was beyond lucky to have kept his eye. My boys certainly kept the doctors and nurses busy there. His next drama was when he caught his thumb in a caravan door; it was hanging by a thread. At the hospital they did a magnificent job and stitched it back onto his hand.

Tyson and Shane are close in years and were especially fond of each other growing up. They still are, in fact. They would do everything together and, like me and my brothers before them, they shared a love of feathered things. From our home in Styal, Tyson and Shane would think nothing of walking nine miles to Chelford Market to watch the chickens being sold, and nine miles back again. It's beautiful countryside to walk in.

Hughie is the youngest son on one side of my family. As a boy he was a little fat thing with long hair and he lived off pie, chips and gravy. The fact that everyone was always giving him sweets didn't help matters much, either. His hair grew so long and thick he could have given Rapunzel a run for her money. It was like a cloak around his shoulders and all the way down his back.

Hughie was always trying to please. I used to say to him 'You are going to turn out the best of all your brothers.'

'Do you really think so, Dad?' he beamed.

When he was eleven, the long hair came off. He was tired of getting stick for it. It was sheared off like a lamb's coat and, oddly, it changed his persona immediately. I'm a very sentimental person and hang on to special things, including bits of pottery, ornaments, old cars, and even my first teddy bear! So it should come as no surprise that I still have Hughie's shaved locks wrapped up in newspaper in one of my vintage caravans.

The cutting of those locks was like a reverse version of the Samson and Delilah story. As soon as they were lopped off, not only could he see where he was going at last, but he began to flourish. He discovered boxing, and the weight fell off as he found a new confidence and direction in himself. He had three amateur fights, and in his first fight he knocked out an Irish champion in the first round. As a pro he fought and won seven times, five by way of knockouts, with only one loss.

Hughie is an excellent bare-knuckle fighter. I call him 'The Smiling Assassin'; behind those beautiful teeth is a demon with a bazooka on each hand.

Tyson and his three brothers like to regroup at the farm. It reminds them of the days they used to roam the green fields and hills of Cheshire, making dens, setting up swings over streams, a time of freedom never to be repeated. As I write, Tyson has been staying here for the last ten days. It's lovely to see the place have such a positive effect on him. It's a raggle-taggle lifestyle here, in no way similar to the good life they lead up in Morecambe, but it is the one he was brought up with.

On the other side of my family, Chantal and I have two sons; Roman and Tommy. Roman is my second youngest son and Tommy's older brother. Roman, like Tyson, has suffered the most from depression. I often worried about him when he was growing up and would go over to see him most weekends to lift his spirits.

Once again boxing came to the rescue. When Tyson won the heavyweight world title again, this time from Wilder, Roman was hugely inspired. He said, 'If Tyson can do it, then so can I.' He shaved his weight down to fourteen stone. He's now turned professional and has already won some impressive matches. I'm really proud of how he now has a positive outlook and has settled into life.

Tommy is the youngest of the bunch. As a kid he was often consumed with self-doubt, wondering where his life was going, watching everybody else doing well. He never felt like he was making headway. When he was three, I bought him a pair of yellow boxing gloves and some pads.

'What do you want for Christmas, Tommy?' I'd say, and without hesitation he said, 'A punchbag and some gloves and headgear, please Dad.' Even though my two youngest sons are from a different mother, the boxing DNA is still inside them.

As a boy Tommy had an enormous nose and I named him after his grandfather Tommy Johnson who had an even bigger conk; he was a lovely guy, but all you could focus on when it was coming towards you was the size of his nose! Tommy is the ugly duckling who grew up to be a swan. Nowadays he has the looks of a Hollywood leading man and the manners of a Victorian gent.

Tommy idolizes his big brother and is very proud of his

achievements in the ring. He once asked me, 'Do you think I'll ever be anything?' and I said, 'Yes I do. But what is it that you would like to be, son?' He gave me a beaming smile and said, 'I'd like to be a boxer like Tyson.'

Boxing brought us all together. It kept us together too. When I went to prison for the last time, Roman and Tommy were only thirteen and eleven years old respectively. I needed somebody to guide them for the rest of their formative years and I turned to my younger brother Peter and asked him to bring them up as his own. And that's exactly what he did. He shaped them into decent fighters and took care of them outside of the ring. For that I am forever grateful.

Everybody wants a piece of Tommy Fury now, he's incredibly busy with TV work. He deserves it, that kid used to ride his bike in all weathers on the twenty-mile round trip to the gyms in Moston and Collyhurst. He sparred with big heavyweight guys at Peter's gym when he was as young as fifteen. He was constantly getting black eyes and broken ribs, but he proved himself.

Tommy is an up-and-coming professional boxer with a record of nine fights, nine wins, four by way of knockout. His school said he would never achieve much, but he has proved them all wrong.

He has a lovely manner too. You'll know this if you watched him in the reality show *Love Island*. He was real throughout the series and always wore his heart on his sleeve. I'd never heard of it before, but I watched his series twice and didn't miss an episode. His looks and TV fame, plus his recent fight with YouTuber-turned-boxer Jake Paul, have made him a a really successful young man.

My lads may be tough as titanium but they've kind hearts and have all been brought up with good manners. Leading up to the fight with Jake Paul in 2023, Tommy was struggling from all the attention he was getting; he felt as if he had the weight of the world on his shoulders. There was so much talk about who was going to win; what round would a knockout occur? So many column inches filling the newspapers with different speculations. The bookies' odds were ever changing; celebrities, current boxers and former champions waded in with their take. Tommy was only young and, with all this media attention, he began to doubt himself. He started listening to some of the negative talk. When part of your income involves your continued presence on social media, it's hard not to come across the doubters. Maybe there were traces of that old Fury paranoia, but Tommy felt that everybody doubted his ability to beat Paul. He'd never been exposed to this kind of scrutiny in his whole life.

We'd trained hard for the fight with a view to sparking Paul out. There is nothing like preparing your son for battle, it's a lovely close feeling you share, building him up and giving him self-belief. The trust between coach and fighter is one thing, but father and son is a whole other dimension. I felt very proud of him.

Even with sixteen-ounce gloves on, Tommy was knocking

out some of his sparring partners, so if Tommy could keep it together, Jake Paul was in trouble. But as the time rolled on toward the 26 February fight, I could tell something was not right in my boy's head.

One day he turned up and said, 'What training are we going to do today, Dad?'

I said, 'We're not going to do any physical training today.'

'Then what are we going to do then?'

'We're going to work on your mind, Tommy. You're definitely fit enough; if you can run an hour without stopping, which you can, then you can go twelve rounds in the ring. The rest is all in your head. So what we're going to have, from now on, is three mental conditioning sessions a week.

'It's all about mindset. If you have a doubt in your head about your ability to beat this kid, your brain starts imagining you losing, and unless you are actively fighting that self-talk, that's exactly what it will deliver come the evening of the fight. So you need to tell yourself that you've got more talent than Paul in your little finger, remind yourself that you come from a fine boxing lineage, and that you've got great power in those fists.'

He nodded gravely.

'This is the biggest fight of your life. It's not the man you have to beat, because you can easily beat him; it's whether you can cope with the mental stress of it all – people doubting you, telling you that you should change your name . . . It's only fun and games and trash-talk, but it's playing on your mind.'

Tommy smiled. 'You know what, Dad, you've never doubted me.'

And I said to him, 'A man with your ability and strength can do anything. If you can get your head right, then you're in a one-horse race. Those men you spar with every day could make short work of Jake Paul if they weren't under pressure. And you're also under no pressure.'

'How do you mean?' he said.

'How can there be pressure when you know you've got everything to beat him with? He's the one under pressure because he's second-rate compared to you, and he knows that. He's throwing mental abuse at you because he can't win with anything else; that's his one and only ace card. If you let that stuff into your head and melt on the day with it, you don't deserve the win.'

He looked despondent.

'Now, imagine you were told you had just three months to live, with your lovely family and everything going for you. That would be pressure. Compare this with your situation, you've got a few rounds with a guy with inferior skills to you, and you're being paid over a million pounds for it. That's fun, it's not pressure.

'Remember when I was stood in the dock waiting for the judge to sentence me for life, twenty-five to thirty years? That was pressure,' I told him.

Tommy nodded. He thought it over and his face began to unknit itself.

So now, during the run-up to my son Tommy's fight

against Jake Paul in Saudi Arabia, I watched in admiration as he calmly handled the trash-talking Yank and his insults. Tommy responded with a measured, courteous demeanour that I can only dream of. He's a credit to himself and to Chantal and me.

I'd do anything for my boys. I would happily have taken Tommy's place and fought Jake Paul on his behalf. But part of being a parent is doing your best to guide your children and then standing back and watching them try their best. It can be heart-breaking, and when a child of yours suffers, you're right there suffering with them. But in the end Tommy handled it all just fine.

On that night of the fight, Tommy prevailed, winning a points decision with a display of panache far superior to the American's style.

The wisdom you dish out as a father is vitally important. When I was a little lad, my dad used to say, 'Accept the present, accept the situation you're in and the cards you've been dealt.'

My father was the closest person to me. If I could have died for him, I would have done. Before he passed at the age of sixty-six, he said to me, 'Your mind can get you in a lot of trouble, son. Yes, I'm on my way out, but look at the fun I've had. I've lived in the best times, the best decades, and done so with a great sense of freedom. I've enjoyed my life, all sixty-six years of it. There are young kids that die every day who never make it anywhere near that age.

'Don't worry, we'll meet again one day. So pull your socks up, son, you've got a lot of work to do, and a big family to take care of.'

My dad was the bravest man in death. His last words are so clear in my head. 'I've had a brilliant life, I've got some good sons, a good wife, and there are lots of people that I love who I'm looking forward to meeting again on the other side. All that remains for me to say is, look after your mother.'

It's the examples that we set through life as parents that help determine the success of our children in their adult lives. Children are so easily scarred by our actions, and I regret them seeing me losing my temper and the violence that was a part of their childhood. I said to my boys, 'Learn from my mistakes, you don't need to make them again. I fought those battles so you don't have to.'

I respect everybody. If I see you stuck, I'll try and help you, but I am also that animal which, if you pull its tail, it will tear you to pieces. When I look back on my life, I cringe when I think of some of the stupid things I have done, like the time I was speeding down the Derby Road in a sports Cortina doing 120 miles an hour in a 40 mph zone and a car appeared towing a caravan and I drove in one side of it and out the other. I wanted to push the boundaries and I suppose I did these things to feel alive, but it was also because I felt worthless. On reflection, I realize I had a death wish. It's not just the person who is at war with himself who gets burnt, it's the people who are closest to him who also suffer. As I write this, I've turned fifty-eight and I am *finally* beginning to mellow, but it's been a long time coming! There is no father on earth who is prouder of his sons than me, they are everything to me, my entire world.

One of the most painful things

about that period after 2011,

when I was sent to jail, was

that I could no longer be

by Tyson's side.

12

The Rise, Fall & Rise
of the Gypsy King

All roads lead to the big TF. Without him there's nothing.
He's always been a good kid, always understanding; in fact,
I think Tyson knows me better than anyone else. He's one
of the main cogs in the Fury family wheel. The night that
Tyson was born is something I'll never forget. It was August,
the baby was due in seven weeks' time. My wife and I had
had problems with previous births. Hearing that she had
gone into labour, I left work and went straight to the
hospital. It was a foul night of thunder and lightning, rain
pouring down as if it was the end of the world. Again there
were complications for my lad; Tyson had been born
massively premature and weighed only a pound. He was
small enough to fit into the palm of my hand.

The doctors said he wouldn't make it, but I saw something completely different, a little warrior with a glint in his eye and his fist held up, as if he was ready to take on the world. And then I experienced a strange feeling that radiated through me like sunshine; it was lovely and I just knew that he was going be better than all right. I said to the doctor, 'That boy is special, he is going to live and he's going to be almost seven foot tall, weigh twenty stone, and one day he's going to be the champion heavyweight of the world, mark my words.' When a Gypsy gets a funny feeling in his stomach, you should always listen to them: the chances are they'll be right.

As he grew up, there were problems for the first four years. He kept overheating and suffering delusions; Tyson would have terrifying hallucinations that lions, monsters and demons were trying to eat him. Amber and I would pack him in ice and rush him to hospital. I started to take him outside for the natural medicine of fresh air. Once, I took him to a golf course. I was mucking around with a golf club, and trying to put a ball in the hole, when the president of the club appeared in the distance. It must've been a strange sight to him, seeing a man with a two-year-old child on a golf course. He started shouting and walking towards me, so I picked up Tyson and legged it. I tried to jump over a ditch but the bank gave way beneath me and I landed with all my twenty stone on my baby son's leg and snapped it. It sounded like a dry stick being broken. I took him home, he was shaking and sobbing in my arms.

Naturally his mother was fuming, and I was devastated. It was one of the most painful experiences of my life, never mind for my poor son.

How could you get this wrong? I asked myself. *How can a father break his own child's leg?*

'You can see the bone sticking out of his leg!' screamed Amber.

I hung my head in shame. 'You're absolutely right. I'm a misfit and not capable of being a father,' I agreed.

We took him to hospital where they performed emergency surgery on the limb. It haunted me seeing his little leg with a steel bolt through it. For me there is nothing worse than causing pain to one of my sons, intentional or not. Thirty-three years on, it still brings a tear to my eye when I think of it.

Over the next six weeks, Tyson wore a kind of protective pot on his leg. It didn't stop him from crawling around the house at speed or drawing boxing gloves. After this traumatic event, I'm glad to say the rest of Tyson's childhood was smooth as milk. We'd buy dogs from *Loot*, a local ads newspaper, where you could buy *anything* from a lobster pot to an Alsatian puppy. I remember one advert read 'black-and-white TV, will swap for colour TV'. That cracked me up, the sheer brazen cheek of it! At one point we had around fifteen dogs. And we took good care of them too. One thing the Furys have in common is we love our animals.

The boys roamed through nature as if they were born

to it. They had a good life. Some locals used to say we Furys on the farm were like the family out of *The Darling Buds of May*. I would sometimes take the boys to car auctions. Every Thursday, when we lived further up north, we'd go to an auction house in Haslingden where the boys would eat all the cheese pies there – they were delicious! It was a simple life.

Tyson was eleven years old when he decided he wanted to take up boxing. Me, I didn't want him to go down that route, so I gave him no encouragement whatsoever. But he was determined to do it and he found an amateur gym on the other side of Wythenshawe; a six-mile walk there and back. It was run by a guy called Steve Egan, better known as Jimmy.

So, Jimmy Egan takes one look at Tyson and his footwork and gives me a call. 'John, you might want to come and have a look at your boy.'

I said, 'I'm too busy working to put food on the table.'

He says, 'No, I mean it, come and have a look, your kid is going to be the future champion of the world.' Jimmy was so impressed that he 'carded' him that night; that's to say, he signed Tyson's medical card, giving him permission to fight as an amateur after watching him just once.

Tyson took to boxing like a duck to water, he was a pure natural. His speed and natural agility for a boy his size were unheard of; he moved just like a middleweight. He was absolutely certain that one day he was going to be heavyweight champion of the world. I certainly didn't disagree with him. He dedicated what remained of his childhood to boxing, training most nights. While his friends went to parties, Tyson continued to train in all weathers, day in and day out. For him it wasn't a big gamble, he knew where he was going and he dedicated every fibre in his body to getting there.

Tyson would put my old boxing gear on, settle on the couch and watch boxing DVDs that he'd found at the car boot sale. He was obsessed, which is exactly what you need to be if you are going to become champion of the world in *any* discipline. It wasn't a sacrifice for him, he enjoyed it. The difficult thing was finding people who were prepared to spar with him; at the age of fifteen, he already stood at six foot five. As he got better and better as an amateur, I would drive Tyson to Huddersfield and Leicester, so he could spar with decent fighters. One of these was Mark Hobson, who was getting ready to fight the future world cruiserweight and heavyweight champion, David Haye.

As an amateur, even with big eighteen-ounce gloves on, Tyson was knocking big men wearing headguards down on the canvas, and that was in training. Eight fights in as an amateur, and he was picked for the British team; it was an astonishingly quick journey. Tyson's amateur career took him all over the world and I did my best to see as many of his fights as possible, however, after travelling solo on a particularly nasty plane journey with the worst turbulence imaginable – people screaming that they were going to die, the plane being tossed around in the heavens like a tin can – I promised myself I would never fly again. So to attend Tyson's European fixtures, I had to climb in the car a few days before and would happily drive across Europe to wherever the venue was.

As an amateur, Tyson won thirty-one fights with two losses. When he turned professional at the age of twenty, there was no shortage of suitors who knew all about this boy wonder and who were looking to represent him. One of them was Don King. I remembered the acrimonious parting that Mike Tyson had had with the motormouth King, and politely declined his offer. My brother Hughie took over training duties from Jimmy Egan, and every day Tyson would train in an icy shed next to Hughie's trailer. Under Hughie's stewardship, Tyson would go on to win both the British and Commonwealth heavyweight titles.

One of the most painful things about that period after 2011, when I was sent to jail, was that I could no longer be by Tyson's side. My brother Peter, who was and is a brilliant coach, had taken over his nephew's training duties from Hughie. Finally, the opportunity to fight Klitschko had presented itself. Unbeknown to the British public, Tyson was regularly experiencing bouts of depression; by the time the good news came, his weight had ballooned to twenty-five stone and he had become indifferent to the announcement he had worked so hard to hear since his mid-teens: 'Wladimir Klitschko vs Tyson Fury'.

On the night of 28 November 2015, the fight billed as

'Collision Course' took place in Düsseldorf. Having slimmed right down, my son gave the audience a masterclass in boxing. Wladimir Klitschko, the long-reigning champion, just couldn't get a handle on him. Tyson was too quick, slippery and clever; at best, all the stricken old Ukrainian could do was fire off a few tired jabs. Tyson won on points and became the new heavyweight champion of the world, and now had three of the four world title belts (World Boxing Organization, World Boxing Association and International Boxing Federation).

But what should've been a triumph became a void. A man who devotes his life to climbing a mountain will eventually reach the top, but unless there's a plan in place to climb another mountain after, or he has something else lined up to challenge him, he's going to slide straight back down that mountain into apathy or worse. Tyson suffers from a condition once called 'manic depression', but these days it's known as 'bipolar syndrome', where everything in his emotional life is more extreme – he feels more intense highs but also darker lows, so his fall down the mountain wasn't just dramatic, it was epic. Not since Roberto Durán's *'no mas'* capitulation to Sugar Ray Leonard in their second fight, or Mike Tyson taking a bite out of Evander Holyfield's ear, had anything shocked the sporting world like Tyson's fall from grace after his victory over Klitschko.

Tyson's weight ballooned to twenty-eight stone, made worse by his attempts to drink himself to death. He was also taking a lot of cocaine, which was contributing to him having almost daily panic attacks. He was lost in himself and couldn't see the value in anything any more, including his family and staying alive. One night he tried crashing his car into a motorway bridge, but at the last minute stopped himself, remembering that it was his duty to be around as a father to help his kids grow up. He wasn't going to be much use to them six feet under.

I remember before the Klitschko fight asking Tyson what he was going to do once he had the heavyweight title. He answered me, 'I will probably get depressed. Whether I win, lose or draw this fight, I'll probably never box again.'

I said, 'But son, you've worked your whole life for this moment.'

Tyson believed the bigger the high, the greater the low, and that's the price that had to be paid. He spiralled out of control and didn't care when his belts were taken away from him; he'd go off and disappear on a bender for days on end. His poor wife, Paris, stuck by him through thick and thin, even though I know there are times when she almost packed her and the kids' bags. Sometimes, she used to pull him out of alleyways when he was passed out. All the principles that mattered to my son, like avoiding drugs, he abandoned in order to hurt himself. He began to feel the paranoia my father had so often experienced, thinking he was going blind or that his family were turning against him. He had been stripped of his belts and titles in 2016 and his licence to box had been revoked.

For two years I lived in fear of taking the call that told

me Tyson was dead by his own hand; I'd become tense every time the phone rang.

He was now reduced to hiding in the house and peeking out of the curtain thinking people were after him. The last straw was when he insisted on being taken to hospital because he was convinced he was having a heart attack. It was a panic attack. He was offered pills but turned them down. Depression never goes away, but it can be dealt with. Tyson tried to self-medicate his black dog with beer and illicit drugs.

One Halloween night, dressed as a skeleton, he was getting drunk in town, when he caught his reflection in a bar-room mirror; still wearing the mask, drinking beer through the nylon netting. He had an epiphany and asked himself: *Why are you around all these people? Do you really want to be here instead of being with your family at home having quality time?*

That night he returned home, went upstairs to his room, and took off the skeleton suit. He was down on his knees in the darkness, snot and tears running down his face, praying for help. He asked the Lord to show him the way back to the light. He then felt a weight tangibly lift from his shoulders. He called out to his wife Paris and told her, 'Tomorrow I start to turn my life around.'

He'd told her this many times and naturally she didn't believe him. But the next day felt *different*. Tyson put on his running gear and went for a jog. He didn't get very far, no more than a few hundred yards, but it didn't matter;

on his phone he'd just seen a YouTube video of Deontay Wilder, the current WBC world heavyweight champion, writing him off: 'Tyson Fury will never be back.' It became the catalyst for Tyson's recovery, and he took it as a personal challenge to prove everyone – particularly Wilder – wrong. It was all the rocket propellant he needed to light him up and push him on with refreshed purpose. He had a new peak to climb, one that would involve losing a mountain of weight.

Tyson left his uncle Peter as his coach, and instead found a young lad called Ben Davison to train him. Ben had never trained a high-profile boxer before but Tyson was ready to give him a shot. His shake-up also involved switching to a new promoter, adding Frank 'Magic Man' Warren to his team. The road to recovery was paved with sweat and tears, and his ultimate destination was a station called 'Wilder', but he would have to stop at a few tune-up waypoints en route. Sefer Seferi was a piece of cake; the Albanian quit on his stool after round four. Tyson looked as if he was enjoying himself, he was in the flow, his panache and mischief back in spades. His next fight was against Francesco Pianeta, a six-foot-five-inch southpaw. It went the full ten rounds.

When the news broke that Tyson would fight Deontay Wilder in Vegas on 1 December 2018, I was mad as hell. That was my way of expressing a father's love and fear for his son. A fully fit Tyson could beat Wilder every day of the week, but this was too much too soon for a fighter who had been out of the ring for thirty-one months. I told him that he could get brain damage and then who would look after his children? I appealed to him to look at the two boxers he had just beaten and then consider Wilder, who was at a completely different level. *This is suicide*, I kept thinking, *and not just career suicide*. 'He'll kill you,' I said finally.

I felt it might be dangerous in a mental sense as well as physical; after all, having won the heavyweight title from Wladimir Klitschko, Tyson had descended into a dark abyss of self-loathing and purposelessness. What if, after clawing his way out of the abyss, he lost again? I just didn't think he was ready to face down the biggest knockout merchant in the history of boxing. At least not yet.

Long before Tyson opened his heart about suffering depression, and he became a national treasure, he was viewed with suspicion by ordinary Britons for some of the non-PC things he had said. What people fail to realize is that when he made those less than savoury comments, he was a very sick man inside his own head. Perhaps my son's outspokenness had something to do with the absence of any fanfare over his victory against the Ukrainian heavy-weight champion. No crowds gathered at the airport to hail their countryman's return; there was no open-top bus parade through the centre of Manchester.

Now, still recovering mentally after his nervous break-down, he was going to be like a lamb to the slaughter, chopped down by that right-hand bomb of Wilder's.

Undeterred by my protestations, Tyson went ahead with the fight, and though it pained me to do this, true to my word I did not speak to him in the weeks leading up to his departure for America.

The expectation at ringside was that Tyson would get knocked out within the first four rounds. In the first round Tyson tied up Wilder, did an Ali shuffle, then landed a nice jab. Wilder's eventual response was to throw a heavy left hook to Tyson's chin that made everyone go silent. There was a reason he was unbeaten over forty fights, thirty-nine by way of knockout.

Over the next few rounds, Ben Davison was unbelievably cool, and advised Tyson not to 'get greedy'; there was more to be gained in tiring Wilder out rather than just landing shots of his own. Increasingly, Wilder was over-focused on detonating his famous right-hand bomb, and in the fourth round he hyperextended his arm. In the seventh round Tyson reasserted himself with a right cross against Wilder's chin and a brilliant left-right combo to the champion's head. Come round nine, Wilder seemed out of ideas, until he pinned Tyson in the corner and unleashed four hooks, one of which connected and knocked the Gypsy King to the floor for the count.

By five he was up on his knees and ready to roll again. Far from running away for the rest of the round, Tyson took the fight straight to Wilder, throwing three great shots. But Wilder was far from done; in the twelfth round, he burst out of his corner and unleashed a killer right followed by a left hook that nearly took Tyson's head off and sent him violently crashing to the floor. I winced as I saw his head bounce off the canvas. At the count of six, I thought it was all over, as my son lay flat-out on the canvas, then suddenly he opened his eyes and seemed to realize where he was and the importance of the moment; by nine he was back on his feet and vigorously nodding his head to signal to the referee he was okay to carry on fighting. He ended the final round in style and, come the final bell, Tyson had every reason, despite his two knockdowns, to believe that he had done enough to win. He was wrong, it ended with a draw. I was super-proud of him.

The second fight against Deontay Wilder, which took place on 22 February 2020 in Nevada, managed to narrowly miss the World Health Organization's declaration of a global pandemic the following month. Tyson switched coaches from Ben Davison to 'SugarHill' Steward. SugarHill is nephew of the famous Manny Steward, who'd steered the careers of so many world champions, including Wladimir Klitschko, Tommy Hearns and, many years earlier, Tyson Fury. SugarHill focused on building body strength to achieve a Kronk-style knockout through heavy punching. It certainly worked.

Tyson always takes punches better with a bit more weight on him, and for this fight he was considerably heavier than at the first Wilder meeting. In fact, at 256½ pounds, he was over forty pounds heavier than his opponent. There was less counterpunching on Tyson's part in Wilder 2, and more domination of the ring from the word go. Wilder had never been put on his back foot before, and Tyson seemed able to weather some of his best punches and walk through them unharmed. By the end of the first round, it was a bewildered – forgive the pun – Wilder who was sitting in his corner wondering how he was going to survive the rest of this fight.

In the seventh it was all over bar the shouting, as Tyson unloaded combination after combination at the stricken boxer. It was then that Wilder's corner finally threw in the towel and, as it floated to the canvas, a relieved Wilder, despite his attempts to question his corner's decision, limped back to his team. If he'd had a Doberman's tail, it would have been between his legs.

Throughout this second fight, Wilder had been utterly dominated, schooled and humiliated by Tyson. For a time after the fight there was some bad sportsmanship, as he claimed that Tyson had had some form of hardening agent, like plaster of Paris, inside his gloves, but eventually he went quiet, stopped his bitching. Deontay went away to take a long look at himself, reflect on his weaknesses and really work on them. My son was again the heavyweight champion of the world. Against all odds and expectations, the Phoenix had risen again from the flames of his own self-destruction.

These days, Tyson exercises to stimulate his mind. During the pandemic he exercised three times per day, soothing his mind with serotonin rather than taking pills.

He also knows the importance of having a purpose, giving himself short- and long-term goals. He plans lots of things so his diary is busy. Having a routine is important to him too. Being social is also crucial; too much time on his own is dangerous. My son has learnt to appreciate the little things in life, like getting up in the morning and going for a run or playing with his kids. Tyson is very fortunate in that, being a professional sportsman, he has the time and space to keep the demons at bay by keeping fit. Through trial and error he's realized he needs to exercise and be around positive people to keep the blackness at bay.

Having been so close to his own death, he really appreciates just how precious life is.

As far back as I can remember,
a streak of melancholy has
run through me.

13

Black Dog: Depression

There is a history of depression and mental instability in my family. My mother's father certainly suffered from it, as did we all from Granddad's violent mood swings. Some said it was because he had been kicked in the head by a horse. When the army came recruiting for the First World War, his suitability was assessed, but he was turned down because of his pronounced paranoia. It must have been an insult to him that his brothers, both fine boxers, were able to enlist. As a boy I remember being frightened by him, even in 25°C heat he would wear big boots, a trilby hat and a thick Crombie overcoat. I don't think I ever saw him take the coat off, never mind the boots. If you weren't 100 per cent focused on what he was saying, he'd clock you around the ear. 'What was that for, Granddad?' I'd ask.

'It's because I don't like you,' he'd say sternly.

I never could tell if he absolutely meant it or whether deep down in the well of his being, there was a little mischief and irony at play. He could be a lovely man and great company; the problem was that this was only one side of him, and it seemed that at least ten people lived inside his head. His suspicion of others and inability to be given any feedback and take it in good cheer was a real problem. I remember he had a Morris Oxford with a rust problem and, rather than scoring the rust away, scraping it clean and then applying his filler to the now non-leprous area, Fred, my grandfather, just added the filler straight on top of the rust. When somebody who knew about the subject attempted to explain it to him, my grandfather's response was to knock him out cold.

He turned to me, pointed at the disaster zone of his bodged repair effort and growled, 'What do you think of that?'

'Very good, Granddad. I mean absolutely, a top job!' I said in a hurry.

My grandfather on my mother's side wasn't the only one who suffered mental health problems; my own father was not a well man and experienced acute paranoia. He believed that everyone was against him, and sometimes he lost his temper and smashed things up, but never people. My mother, not knowing what was wrong with him, just thought he was being aggressive and so took the fight to him. Eventually, we discovered that he was suffering from schizophrenia and after that he was heavily medicated to help level his mood. My father would be on these pills for the rest of his life. However, what he wasn't aware of was that there was nothing in the tablets. They were placebo meds; they only worked because he believed they helped calm him down, when in fact it was *him* calming himself down. I remember one bank holiday my father ran out of his meds and he was unbearable, it was two days of hell. But we understood he didn't mean the nasty things he was saying, and tried not to take it to heart.

My own black dog

When I'm down, I don't feel like doing anything; nothing interests me. The Celts used to call depression 'the black dog', and I certainly have my share of being bitten. That's a good description, because depression feels like it's gnawing away at your soul. As far back as I can remember, a streak of melancholy has run through me. Some mornings I wake up and for no reason I just feel sad and down with the world. It's as if nothing can make me happy, and the window through which I'm looking is dark and obscure, bereft of any trace of sunlight.

My depression is far worse than I let on. I'm tortured by it almost every day of my life. Only yesterday it was my birthday, and I couldn't find my keys for love nor money. I was supposed to be somewhere attending a dinner that had been organized for the occasion, but losing the keys made me forty-five minutes late and in the end I decided not to bother going out and sacked the whole day off. My head was gone.

I thought to myself, 'Oh well, you're having a bad day, so get your boots on and go for a long walk.' I felt drained and like I couldn't be bothered to do anything, but I've been around for fifty-eight years now, and one thing I do know is that depression hates a moving target. However bad things get, I know that as soon as I put my shoes on and get out the door, the horrible haze which settles over me if I stay indoors begins to vaporize in the fresh air and sunshine.

Depression can make you feel dirty and worthless, like you don't belong anywhere. It makes you feel stiff and awkward with others, tells you things that aren't true; discolouring how you think about yourself. And the longer you entertain its thoughts, the worse it gets. In my case it can hit me at any time. It doesn't look at my calendar and book itself in at a convenient slot. If you allow it to, the black dog can be waiting for you from the first moment you wake up in the morning. When I'm getting on with life, depression sneaks up on me from nowhere and then within twenty minutes my mood can change dramatically and I feel suicidal. 'What's the point of this?' I ask myself. I have noticed that as I get older, the depression is getting harder to shift.

I love walking my dog and being outside as a means of fighting the dark thoughts that enter my head. Outdoors you are among nature, which is soothing, and you meet people with their dogs and have great conversations. Most young people haven't got time for walking because they're too much into their phones and consumed by the virtual life they lead on social platforms.

The danger of tech and social media

I think that when your nose is buried in a phone you are no longer in contact with the reality around you; instead it's a kind of fake world of lies where people pretend to look more wealthy and beautiful than they actually are. There are apps which can make you look thin, or your skin glow more healthily than it does; you can brighten your eyes and reshape your chin. Now what's that all about?

Don't get me wrong, there's plenty of good things about the Internet. For example, I can find out who the third president of the United States was, or I can look at Google Maps to navigate my way to a place I don't know. What's really bad is when kids don't see the light of day because they're locked up in their room looking at an artificially lit screen for hours and hours on end. Then there's hackers, and paedophiles who prey upon the innocent – don't get me started.

When I was a kid, street corners were peppered with children playing games: hopscotch, tag, marbles, conker fights . . . they were riding their Grifters and Choppers without health and safety laws screaming at them from every corner, and they lived for the weekends when they were free to roam wherever their feet or wheels took them.

If you're on Instagram you can accidentally navigate from the photo page into the reels page which is full of moving footage, and the next thing you know it's claimed an hour of your time and you've disappeared down a rabbit hole watching stuff that you'll never remember. It's the same on TikTok. These sites are so *addictive* that our kids are cannibalizing their own childhoods.

I only use these smartphones for information. Fortunately I'm of an age where I can still put them down as I wasn't reared on them. I read in the Bible when I was a teenager that one day in the near future there would be an explosion of intelligence, and I believe these phones are part of this prediction and like loaded guns; every time a young person picks one up, they are playing Russian Roulette with their mental health, and – by the time they put the phone down – there is every chance that somebody will have made them feel small, diminished, like they're failing or they're ugly. These phones and the companies that tailor advertisements around your browsing habits are only as smart as you allow them to be. You've got to have enough willpower to be able to say, 'You know what, I've had enough of that phone today,' and then you put it somewhere safe and leave it. The world is a beautiful place, and you must dedicate yourself to exploring as much of it as you can, rather than worshipping a hunk of metal and glass that is stealing your time.

I don't want to sound like a conspiracy theorist, because I'm not one of those, but for the powers that be it's better that we don't use our initiative and are more like sheep than dogs following our own separate scent. This was never more apparent than during the pandemic and the lockdown caused by COVID-19. What struck me then was that the population of this country, and indeed many countries all over the world, were under the complete control of their government. I find it strange that the world is moving at a pace where technology is growing so rapidly that we can't keep up with it; jobs are being rapidly automized – have you noticed that when you go to a supermarket there are fewer and fewer staff on the tills and more self-service machines?

A few years ago, we all had a good moan when the customer services section of companies were automated with voice-activated software, giving you options of which buttons to press on your phone to take you to a different section of the company. Now the technology of 'bots' is so advanced that we no longer know whether it is a human or not answering the phone when we call our bank or service provider.

The more people lose their jobs to automation, the more they are dependent on the state for handouts. Have you noticed how many pubs are closing down (according to a recent survey more than 7000 over the last decade), traditionally the very places where people got together to discuss necessary social change and life itself? Public houses, once known as taverns, have existed for over a thousand years or more. People in numbers are powerful, they ask painful questions, they come to an agreement or disagreement. Like on the issue of mental health. I want people talking, discussing how to address the causes of their problems, not necessarily seeking a prescription that might just cover the pain like a plaster over a wound. Medication does help, and you must take it if you need it, but I can't help but feel we need more spaces to come together and heal together.

Can you imagine what the drug companies would say if there was suddenly a natural cure for today's disorders of anxiety and depression? It perfectly suits the powers that be for us to be drifting along in a haze of lithium or Prozac, like numb zombies of clay easily shaped into whatever we are required to be. I believe it's the big pharmaceutical, tech and oil companies who influence government policy, and it is they who control the political narrative. I know I have very little control over these big companies, but my one defence is to have an old analogue Nokia phone which has none of my details on it, and the fact I owe nobody any money so there's no bank that can pass my details on or control me with loans, and finally, I don't take any medication that will fund the jobs of these drug companies. For these three reasons I consider myself exceptionally fortunate.

Man will destroy himself; he's become too clever for his own good. Don't get me wrong, there's some wonderful people working in healthcare and overall they do more good than bad, but I'm talking about people at the heads of industry, the titans, the real decision-makers.

It could be you on a street corner

It's easy for young people to get lost in today's system. All of us are closer to sleeping rough beneath an underpass than we might realize. A couple of wrong decisions, or an unexpected tragedy which causes you to spiral into poor mental health, can be followed by the loss of a job, house repossession and, before you know it, you're on the street. That might seem a bit dramatic to you, but when I see somebody outside a supermarket or on the street corner with a begging bowl, I stop and talk to them, I want to hear their stories. In today's society, if you are homeless and don't have any money, you're looked upon as untouchable, somebody who deserves to be ignored and who's not worth speaking to. There seems to be no space for the poorer person any more.

To people I see begging on the streets, I try to convince them that they're worth more than this, that the human being is a species that is bred to work, and when it doesn't, it is going against its own inbuilt system. 'Work,' I tell them, 'gives you money, but it also gives you a sense of satisfaction in a job well done and self-respect; whereas sitting on your arse in a drizzly archway waiting for somebody to take pity on you doesn't.

'There are opportunities out there,' I say, 'if only you look for them. You can change your life in as little as six months with a little luck and determination, but the way you're going at the moment, are you going to live and die in a doorway?'

Recently, as I pulled up in my car outside my local Sainsbury's, I saw a guy sat cross-legged in the rain outside the entrance, his hat empty but for a few coins, filling with rain.

I said to him, 'I'm going to go and buy you something to eat.'

He said, 'I don't want any food, can I just have the money, please?'

'I'm not giving you money so you can spend it on drugs. Why are you sat here in the rain, catching your death of cold, while that dealer is driving around in a warm, expensive-looking car. Every time you give him money, you make his life easier while yours gets harder, just remember that.

'How old are you, about thirty-five? Get a grip on yourself, man. There are good people out there who can help you get sorted, if you'll meet them halfway.'

The next time I went to Sainsburys he was gone. I'm a big believer that we were put on this earth to help one another. Sometimes I get this voice in my head regarding certain people that I feel I must speak to, and I feel much better knowing I have just convinced someone who's down on their luck to try and find hope in themselves and to climb back up off the canvas. I appreciate it sounds like I'm giving them tough medicine.

I see people in their fifties, sixties and seventies out walking for the same reason as me; they walk to feel better and keep their mental health balanced. Life is about communicating with others face to face, and going for a walk with your dog gives you an excuse to break the ice with other dog owners. I met a delightful couple with a spaniel, who I walked alongside with my dog for about a mile, chatting about everything under the sun, including the subject of depression. Just moving around and talking to like-minded people in a beautiful place can lift your mood. You think to yourself, 'I'm not that weird, after all, everybody gets depressed. It's just some people are more prepared to be honest about it than others.'

Instead of allowing my low mood to ruin the whole of my birthday yesterday, I took the pressure off myself and went walking out in the sunshine. I thanked everybody for planning the day for me and said, 'Listen guys, I really appreciate it, but I'm going to take a rain check, I need a bit of time to myself today.' The thought of all that noise and all those crowds of people just put me into a place of further despair and anxiety. I wasn't in the mood for it, so I went for my walk and by the time I returned from a six-mile ramble, I felt much better.

Maybe I am being unnecessarily hard on myself, but nobody wants to be around somebody who's not firing on all four cylinders. A negative mood can rub off on others around you and ruin their day, so if I'm not jolly and happy, I keep away from people. That's what I've always done, I suppose there's no point changing now. As a lad, my mum could read me very quickly. Just a mannerism might give me away, a heaviness in my gait or a distant look in my eyes would signify the black dog had come to stay in me. 'You having a bad day today, son? Don't worry,' she'd say.

I love the evenings because I feel like I've survived the mental difficulties of the day. After my walk, I listened to a podcast called 'The Lion of Judah' and finally fell asleep at three in the morning. Some days you just can't help how are you feeling and you have to listen to your inner wisdom telling you what you really need, because that's your true compass. In my case it's always the fresh air I use as my sword and shield against the legion of black dogs that come looking for me.

Declare war on depression

Depression for me is a war I have to fight every day, a cross I've been given to bear. Every day I address my tormentor, and tell him: 'Right, Mr Depression, listen to this. I beat you when I was in jail in an eight-by-six-foot cell, locked in for twenty-three hours per day, and I'll beat you on the outside. Outside it's a fair fight, I'm on home ground and I'm going to win every time.'

But believe me, he puts up a good fight!

I only use the hospital when I'm seriously ill or I have a broken limb, otherwise I avoid doctors like the plague and have never had a physician keeping a regular eye on me. Being a lone wolf has not always been helpful, as it's meant that I've depended only upon myself and dealt with everything on my own, including depression. I suppose I lock myself away when I'm feeling like this, because I don't want people to see the worst of me and what I'm going through, particularly my sons. Because for them to see me diminished would take away their perception of me as their rock, and until my dying breath I want to be there for them in every way I can be. If I was to allow them to be a support for me and reach out on those very dark days, it might change their view.

I'm glad that Tyson has got proper positive emotional support around him when he's deeply depressed, people that he can rely on. At least one of us has got it right. I'm probably being unnecessarily protective of them boys, a bit stubborn and old-fashioned. But that just about sums John Fury up.

Some days I look at things and ask myself, 'What's the bloody point of it all?' and I start thinking of all the people I love who have already passed and will be waiting for me on the other side. When I start heading down this morbid track, a voice inside of me – my inner wisdom – fights back and says: 'Come on, stop thinking like that, you've got a family that needs you and you've still got responsibilities. So put your steel armour on, get your head together, you're a long time dead.' That usually talks me around and gets me out of the door.

Exercise, no matter how thin, fat, in- or out-of-shape you are, is good for your mental health and good for your soul. When we exercise, our body releases endorphins; these are one of the feel-good chemicals which your brain releases as a reward for kicking up a sweat. Not only does exercise make you look better, it makes you feel better too.

During the pandemic, Tyson kept himself mentally in check by vlogging an exercise routine with Paris to hundreds of thousands of his followers on Instagram every day. He never missed a single day, partly because he didn't want to let people down, and also because it was a necessary discipline to keep himself both physically and mentally fit. On top of this he would go cycling and for a run all in one day. The result of that massive natural production of endorphins was only positive, and allowed him to get through what otherwise would've been a dark and deeply frustrating time. Personally I like hitting a bag and going jogging to keep fit.

Depression hates a moving target

I want to be an advocate for mental health, and to inspire people with depression that you can still have a life. What brings me round from my depression is being useful to those that are suffering and who get in touch with me for advice. I tell them, 'Get a good pair of hiking boots and get out there, just don't sit inside on your own, stewing and making it worse.'

We are now beginning to understand mental imbalance, as science gets to grips with the human brain and understands the chemicals it produces. When there are deficiencies in the release of hormones responsible for keeping our spirits afloat, like serotonin or dopamine, the mind goes into a numb place. It's proven that exercise causes your body to release dopamine which is an energizer. One of the first things that depression brings on is apathy, a disinterest in life, and a generally *can't be bothered* attitude. But when you've got energy from exercise, you just feel good.

Anti-depression techniques

I find that the best way to cut depression down before it grows any bigger is to expose it, and that is what happens when you speak to someone like-minded who knows what you're going through. It's when you don't talk to others and try and suppress the dark way you're feeling that it begins to control your life. My son is six foot nine – they don't come much bigger than him – and yet depression almost killed him.

If you can't get hold of a friend, then try distracting yourself from your thoughts. We are a product of our thoughts, and if we don't fill our brain with positive thinking very quickly, it will find something negative to fix on. If you left me in a room for an hour on my own, I'd soon get to thinking negatively, creating scenarios in my head that weren't real: *the world is against me, it's all one big waste of time, and what is the point of breathing anyway?* I'd even look at Tyson's achievements, and think, *all those plaudits for what, a boxing match? That's nothing.* Some days I even think my own sons are plotting against me. It's at this point I firmly tell myself to stop and check in with reality, whatever that is! *Where's the evidence for what you're thinking?* I ask myself.

I try to meet my monster of depression head-on. He's an ugly bastard. I can't tell you how many times he's kicked my spirit in the balls and told me to pull the plug on life and do everybody a favour. But there's nothing I relish more than a fight, so I refuse to be beaten.

One good thing about getting older is that you have the benefit of hindsight, and the longer you're here the more you realize that these thoughts are just voices, you are worth more and there *will* be sunlight tomorrow, even if there's not a trace of it today. Life moves in cycles, and if we were always in a good mood we wouldn't actually appreciate what a good mood is. The fact is we need the dark to celebrate the light. It's all part of the wheel of life. Not everybody is as mentally strong as I am, perhaps because of the hard life I've come through, and there is no shame in asking for professional help to get you out of a rut and set you back on your feet again. Many people are afraid of the stigma attached to having bad mental health and seeking out someone who can help, but it's always worth trying to do so.

Fight and flight

The world is a wonderful place if only we bother to look for its magic. Think about it; there are so many things you could do in a day – buy a train ticket and go somewhere new; watch a good film; have a good conversation with an interesting person. The bad stuff will present itself to you because the brain is trained to look for the negative, whereas it takes conscious effort to fix your eye on things which will make you happy. Why? Because humans are programmed to be highly sensitized survival creatures; looking over our shoulders, and watching out for things that can hurt us, has kept us modern humans alive for the last 200,000 years. And get this, only 15,000 years ago we were still being hunted by sabre-tooth tigers; so, for most of our time here on Earth, we've needed to read situations pessimistically in order to be aware of the dangers.

This is why our bodies have this inbuilt mechanism called 'fight or flight'. If you're John Fury, you never run away. If only my flight mechanism worked a little bit more efficiently, I might not have been in half the trouble I have been! Fight mode is just another fancy name for the 'red mist', a state in which the body feels less pain, has more strength and is not fully aware of what it is doing. Vikings used to take special hallucinogenic cocktails made from plants to put them in this red mist state when they were in battle. A Viking under the influence was called a 'berserker', which is where the modern word 'berserk' comes from. I'm full of useless information, me!

Your mind is a very complicated thing and can be difficult to control. Some days it doesn't matter how much you have in the bank, or the delightful company that you're sharing, you just feel flat for no good reason. You can be the happiest man in the world one day and the most miserable the next. I know the signs that my mood is sliding; it starts with the seeds of doubt, the voice of depression growing in your mind. It's then I try to make a conscious decision not to spiral into depression. If I can catch it early, I can change my thinking altogether within the space of an hour, either by calling someone I know, or getting my running kit on and tiring myself out with exercise. I try to be my own coach and corner man, cheering myself on, looking at my reflection and saying, 'Come on, Johnny lad, don't let it beat you, you're better than that.' The more that you feed yourself with self-loathing, the quicker the slide into the pit.

There is an old Cherokee saying that in one pocket we have a black wolf of hate, and in the other pocket we have a white wolf of kindness. Which wolf are we going to feed?

A stranger in need

Not long ago I received a call from a young lad who sounded desperate. He sent me a text message with his phone number. So I called him, and he was very quiet on the phone when he answered.

He asked, 'Would Tyson be available if possible for twenty minutes of his time?'

'Tyson's not available, but I'll make sure he sees you when he's back.'

He was quiet for a moment, but I could sense the desperation coming down the phone in the uneasy silence. 'Would it be possible if I could have a few minutes of your time instead?' he asked.

'Where are you?' I said.

'Derby,' he answered.

'I'm on my way.' That night I drove the hour and a half journey from Styal to Derby, probably a little quicker than I might have done ordinarily, but I knew the minutes were precious, and odd as it may sound, I could smell death on the boy. It's a Gypsy thing, but I've often sensed death on individuals who have shortly passed on afterwards.

I met the lad, who turned out to be about thirty. The look in his eye said he'd given up on life. 'You're a mental health sufferer,' I said softly to him. 'Tyson is a mental health sufferer, and I'm a mental health sufferer. The difference with you and me is that I won't let depression beat me, because I know that tomorrow is a new and different day and it can be bright and happy and joyful. You're brightening my world up because I know I can help you get to tomorrow. But I want something from you now.

'I came from Styal to Derby and I didn't know you from Adam. I came here because I knew you needed help. Now, I'd like to make an appointment with you and Tyson in twenty-eight days' time as we're in Sheffield on that day. Can you do that, son? I want to see you with your chin up and smiling, and if you don't have enough money to get to Sheffield, just text-message me and I'll organize you transportation to come pick you up. We'll be here at this address,' I said and wrote it down for him.

'Will you be there?' I asked.

He was smiling a little now, his eyes a little brighter, albeit a small glimmer. And that grip of death that had a few minutes earlier had its black wings around his shoulders had now receded, at least temporarily, into the darkness of the Derbyshire night. Hope is a stronger weapon than despair, if only we can take a rag to it with some spit and polish so we see it shine. Sometimes a glimmer is all you need to get started, just the promise of sunshine to come.

He nodded and said, 'Yes, Mr Fury, I'll be there,' looking at the address I'd written down as if it was Willie Wonka's golden ticket.

Did he turn up at the designated place twenty-eight days later? He certainly did, and he met Tyson and chatted with him and me. And that wasn't the last episode: three months later we saw him again; he was happy, he had a new job and a girlfriend with him. To have helped him get to this point was my sustenance, it felt wonderful. It doesn't happen every day that you get the opportunity to really help somebody flip their situation, but when you do, you not only take great satisfaction in the deed and result, but also you feel a little better about yourself as a human being. I sometimes do speaking engagements, and I often see him in the crowd and we'll chat afterwards. At the last one he revealed, 'Thanks to you, Mr Fury, I'm getting stronger every day, and my wife is now expecting our first child.'

It meant an awful lot to hear that. Most of my life I have felt like a monster, very few people have understood me, and I've cast myself as an exile even amongst the Travelling folk, who are themselves outsiders. I feel guilty for many of the things I've done, but when I can lift someone else up from despair, it gives me a brief respite and escape from my self-loathing.

I don't care what colour you are, where you're from or the language you speak, I've got time for you if I can help you. I know that as someone who has come from a humble background and that has a platform in the world of boxing and beyond, I've been given this platform to try and assist others by sharing the mistakes I've made and really listening to them. There's a big difference between listening and hearing. Hearing is waiting for an opportunity to say your bit, to speak about yourself to make you feel bigger or more important; whereas listening is putting your ego to one side and completely focusing on the other person and their story. And it is so important because, as I've learned the hard way, it's when we don't listen that conversations turn into arguments which then spill over into violence.

The importance of having a purpose

We all need a purpose because without one, what is the point in getting up in the morning? If you were allowed to do everything you wanted to all the time without any challenge in your life, you would get very bored. If all you had to do was play golf at some point, it would lose its appeal. A person is at their happiest when they are positively challenged and can respond to that challenge using this skill and enthusiasm. It doesn't matter whether I'm talking about boxing or learning to be a good chef, it's challenge that counts. Now when Tyson beat Klitschko, he fulfilled a teenage dream that one day he would beat the long-reigning heavyweight champion of the world. It was all he cared about, and he fixed Wladimir Klitschko in his crosshairs and he was going to do everything he needed to make sure he fulfilled his destiny. That crowning night in Munich, when he confounded the plodding champion on what was his eleventh defence of his title, would have made the end of a film, but life isn't a film and there's always another chapter, and Tyson had not planned beyond the fulfilment of his purpose.

I believe there are a great many people walking about depressed who are considering committing suicide, every hour of the day. That's not a life, that's not even an existence, it's purgatory. And it isn't just hard for the individual, it's also people around them who suffer with it as well: your friends, family, whoever you may be with at that time. You can't hide poor mental health, it will always find its way to the surface, however hard you try to cover up. I believe it needs addressing properly, and there should be more done about it; it is very serious.

The problem with men

According to the Samaritans 'middle-aged men are more likely to die by suicide than any other age group.' This particularly affects those from less well-off backgrounds. There are still very high figures among young men who feel disenfranchised and isolated socially. Events like relationship breakdown, or job loss can also lead to self-loathing, and a lack of hope in the future, which have all been known to increase risk of suicide.

In an in-depth survey done by the Samaritans with Network Rail workers, they found that when men believe they're not meeting the gold standard of having a job and providing for their family, they feel a sense of shame and defeat, as if they've lost their manhood. Some respond to their overwhelming desperation by taking their own life. We also know that men respond to stress by taking risks, and/or self-medicating with alcohol and drugs and are less prone to share their pain with another man compared to women.

When relationships break down between a man and wife, or girlfriend and boyfriend and they are parents, it tends to be the men who are separated from their children and this can often trigger feelings of guilt, uselessness and potentially suicide. When you're a dad you have a purpose, a reason for going out in the world and working hard – it's for your kids and missus. But once this purpose is taken away, if it's a menial, unengaging job, it can become like torture and feel like being enslaved, it loses any meaning.

Another interesting finding is that mid-life, once considered as the prime of a man's life as he's likely to be at his highest rung on the employment ladder and earning more than ever, is actually now considered as a time when many men suffer more unhappiness and mental stress, and a feeling of loneliness. When compared to people in their twenties and thirties, guys of a certain generation entering middle age are now caught in a kind of hinterland buffer zone, somewhere between their older, more traditional parents – with stiff upper lips, and the chin-up approach to life – and more idealistic sons who are progressive, more individual, and not afraid to show their emotions. As such, many men are conflicted as to whether they are supposed to be strong and silent like their dads and grandfathers, or whether they're okay to let it out and express themselves. I know which one I belong to – the former: you will not find me having a cry when I watch a Disney film. But my son Tyson is very happy to have a good sob when he's watching *Marley and Me*. Neither way is right or wrong, we're just of different generations and upbringings.

I'm old school, we were brought up rough and tough; you only had a problem if you were dying with a terminal illness. Mental health never came into play as we never had the time to sit around as people do today. I spent all my young days working, so I was much too tired to feel down and depressed; when you are up at five in the morning and get to bed at ten o'clock at night in the summer, and in winter you're working from dawn till dark, there's no time to indulge depression. These days people have probably got too much time on their hands, and you know what they say, 'The devil makes work for idle hands.' Also, most people don't work as hard as we used to, by which I mean that so many jobs are sedentary nowadays that physically they probably don't expend as much energy during the day as we used to.

Having a job not only pays you, it also gives you something to do with your life. After five days' graft during the week, you then appreciate the freedom of the weekend, rather than it being just another two days at the end of the week. Having something to be excited about, something to look forward to regularly is really important; that's why – as kids – we were always happy on Thursday and Friday because it was near the weekend. It is so important to have something to look forward to in life. We should fill our diaries with the things that we want to do and people that make us happy. We only get one crack at life before we get old; we should take ourselves travelling and not spend all our time working. When you book a holiday, part of the enjoyment is the anticipation of what it's going to be like, as well as the memories you make when you actually experience the holiday. Excitement is a good state to be in.

It's the same with having a purpose. It gives you a meaning to be, something to strive for, to train towards, in order to bring the best of yourself out to achieve it. The way to give yourself a purpose is to set yourself a goal that's going to challenge you and reward you once you get there. Humans need to strive, they need to push themselves, solve problems and experience difficulties on the way to achieving their goals. When you don't have a goal, it's like a hunter not having a deer to catch; he loses his purpose.

There are those, of course, who are wired differently from birth, those who are more vulnerable to being depressed, through no fault of their own, but just because of the chemical make-up of their brain, like my son Tyson. Growing up he suffered acutely with depression; it was not something that arrived just after he beat Klitschko.

Every so-called friend
I've ever trusted has let me
down in the end.

14

Stranger Things

Telling fortunes

As my mother got older, we spent a lot of time together. She was more than my mum, she was my best friend. She would say to me, 'Keep away from problems because I can see it coming. I seen it in my dreams.' She told me this the very day before an altercation I had at a car auction landed me in jail with an eleven-year sentence. She could see round corners, my mum, and made a few quid reading fortunes. She was the real thing. Nobody wants to know what's round the corner in their lives, unless it's something really good – that's what we call hope. Muhammad Ali used to tell people he was going to be heavyweight champion of the world one day and it happened. My son Tyson also used to say the same thing, and curiously that happened too. Destiny or positive self-talk and manifestation? Who can say. But to hear that something bad is waiting for you down the road doesn't help anybody; it ends up haunting you for the rest of your life as you wait for it to happen. That's the power of the mind – or destiny, perhaps.

In 1991 I was in Spain. There was a fortune teller and I did my best to avoid her. Even my wife said, 'Do not talk to that woman, don't even look at her.' But the woman had her gaze locked on me and there was no getting away from it. 'Have your fortune read?' she says.

'No thanks, we're Gypsy people ourselves.'

Despite the rebuff, she defiantly hobbled towards us and looked at the missus. 'I tell you any way.' She was Spanish Romani, her skin deep brown and creased as an old boot, her dark eyes glossy as a raven's coat. 'In your life,' she said to my other half, 'you will have a lot of miscarriages.' She was right, there had been many miscarriages. Then the crone studied me carefully, her head tilted like a bird. 'You *are* a strange character. Very bad temper, I see a lot of blood, violence and bars . . . prison.'

She looked back at my wife. 'You will have a son, he will be very famous and very rich.' Then at me, 'Your mother is not doing too well. Not long to live.' I swallowed; my mother was in fact dying of cancer. 'Your father not well man, he going to die.'

'That's enough now,' I said as I trawled my pockets for

some cash. Then I pressed a hundred-peseta note into her palm in the hope it might shut her up. 'Thank you very much.'

She regarded me darkly, 'One more thing, keep your children out of water as one of them will drown.'

I never forgot that disturbing prediction, and when my kids were growing up, I'd say to them, in fact I still do, 'Steer clear of swimming pools, the sea, lakes and rivers. The only water you should come across is the water you brush your teeth with or have a shower in. Everything else that that Gypsy lady said was true, and we can't afford to take any risks.'

Vampires

Not all my travels were tainted by tragedy, far from it. I've always had a fascination with films from Hammer Horror Studios, championed by Peter Cushing and Christopher Lee. Dracula is my all-time favourite story, and follows a Victorian solicitor turned estate agent, Jonathan Harker, as he travels to Romania to meet a mysterious count who wants to buy a large property in England. To reach Dracula's castle high in the Carpathian Mountains, Harker must pass through the forbidding Borgo Pass where he is picked up by a coach and horses. I retraced the last leg of Harker's journey from the Romanian medieval town of Bistriţa, which is very close to Ukraine, up through the stunning 'Borgo Pass', which is actually the Tihuţa Pass, to the elevated spot where the castle would have stood in the book. It's a ruggedly beautiful place, where at night you can hear wolves howling and the wind screaming like Dracula's brides, as it rushes around a nunnery on the top of the mountain.

In Romania the Roma still consult Tarot cards to foretell the future. In remote areas of the country, Romanians are still very superstitious, and use garlic to ward off creatures of the night. During the 1999 solar eclipse, some villages even rang church bells and built huge fires to keep were-wolves at bay. Another more recent story: in 2004, just a hundred miles from the capital Bucharest, two men were arrested for digging up a body, cutting its head off and driving wooden stakes through its ribcage. Apparently, the corpse had turned into a *nosferatu* (vampire) and had been wandering around the village at night.

To the north-east of Romania is the little-known country of Moldova. If visiting Romania had felt like travelling back in time, then Moldova – with its pretty painted monasteries and locals dressed in old-fashioned garb – felt truly ancient. I met plenty of Roma Gypsies here. They had a twinkle in their eye and were quick to gather around me with interest. When I tried to convince them I was of their stock, they would have none of it, pointing to my pale skin. Roma Gypsies originally came from India and are very swarthy. In Romania they are considered something of a plague and blamed for every crime.

There are more bears, wolves and lynx lurking in the

forests of Romania than anywhere else in Europe, and it's all down to one man. Nicolae Ceaușescu was a proper wrong'un; the President of Romania had banned every citizen from hunting these three predators in any of 'his' forests, not because he wanted to preserve them, but because he wanted to hunt them all himself. The dictator's secret police, known as the Securitate, turned families against each other, forcing children to become 'informers' and to report on their parents' political thoughts, installing hidden microphones in their houses. But it was the Roma Gypsies who were the worst off under his rule, as Ceaușescu encouraged the hate crime against them and didn't even recognize their status as a people living in Romania, and in doing so took away from them any kind of human rights.

A few days after meeting the Gypsies in the mountains, I heard a strange story at a little village inn, which illustrated the common view of the Roma. There were a few local types in the corner of the cafe-cum-bar. It was dark in there, there were crimson-coloured rugs on the walls and wooden rafters. We got into conversation and they asked where I had been. They seemed nice enough. I replied I'd been up in the mountains, talking with the Roma. At the mere mention of the word 'Roma' they recoiled in horror. It reminded me of the scene in the Slaughtered Lamb pub, at the start of *An American Werewolf in London*, when one of the American lads asks about the pentagram on the wall, and everything goes deathly quiet.

An old Moldovan man with a leathery face spoke up, his face contorted in disgust, his eyes bright with anger. 'The Roma are evil people.'

'Why?' I asked.

'I'll tell you this much,' he said darkly, 'when the third Antichrist comes to the world, it will be up in those mountains and from among these people.'

Thankfully, the subject changed, and the old-timer asked me what I was doing there. 'I'm on the trail of Dracula,' I said.

His eyes instantly cooled from their Bunsen burner blue. He smiled and said, 'That I can help you with,' and he went on to explain where the roots of the Dracula story came from.

The original inspiration for Dracula, created by Bram Stoker, came from a real man, a warrior prince called Vlad Tepes, more affectionately known as 'Vlad the Impaler'. He came from an area in Romania known as Wallachia, and he is celebrated as a hero in the country today for his success in repelling the Ottoman army in the fifteenth century. Vlad impaled 20,000 Turks on huge wooden stakes; the spike went through the victim's behind, up through the body's organs, and out through the mouth. Vlad's father was called Vlad Dracul. '*Dracul*' literally translates as 'the devil'. Which made him, fittingly, the son of the devil.

I visited the citadel town of Vlad's birthplace, Sighişoara. Perched high on a pinnacle of rock, from which you can see for miles around, it's a place of wilting buildings, black

Me and Tyson at the gym together back in 2006.

Tyson and me celebrating as he beat John McDermott to win the English heavyweight boxing title. Essex, 2009.

Training with Tyson in 2015 ahead of his fight with Ukraine's Wladimir Klitschko.

Tyson showing everyone who is boss and ending Klitschko's reign as champion.

Tyson celebrating with the WBA, IBF, WBO and IBO belts after winning the world heavyweight title. I still have to pinch myself sometimes when I think of all he's achieved.

I've learned to control my temper as I've gotten older but if I hear someone talking rubbish about one of my sons then I'm not afraid to stand up to them. This was at a homecoming event in Bolton after Tyson had become world champion in 2015.

The Furys always praise God in our wins. Tyson and Paris here celebrating after he beat Deontay Wilder and retained the heavyweight title. Nevada, 2021.

Celebrating victory after the WBC world heavyweight title fight between Tyson Fury and Dillian Whyte at Wembley in 2022.

Tommy and me training together in 2022 at Boxpark in Croydon.

Tommy has come a long way since he was the ugly duckling of the family.
He's now a leading man and strong fighter.

Another fighter in the family. Roman fighting Erik Nazaryan
in their cruiserweight bout. London, 2023.

The whole team celebrating Tommy's win against Jake Paul in the
cruiserweight title fight. Riyadh, Saudi Arabia. February 2023.

Training with the boys in Manchester. My son Roman is standing
next to me and Tyson is posing on the floor at the front.

Me and Roman on a beautiful day walking in the Peak District.
There's nothing better for the mind that getting out and hiking in nature.

My son Hughie on the left and my late mother to my right, Tyson on the far right.

Family comes first. Tyson on the left, my late brother James in the middle and my son Hughie on the right.

It's the simple things in life that make me happy. My one indulgence is vintage cars.

cats and narrow cobbled streets. Close to a thirteenth-century clock tower there is a little house that looks like something out of Hansel and Gretel, and above its door hangs the sign of a dragon. It seems an unlikely place for the birthplace of one of history's great monsters.

I don't know what it is about Dracula that resonates with me; maybe it's because he's an outsider. I do like a drop of the red stuff now and again, but I stick to wine rather than blood, and I think that's where the similarity ends.

This quirky, enduring interest of mine in horror films comes directly from my three spinster aunts, collectively named by their brother (my father) as 'the clucking hens'. As I was growing up, Aunts Patchy, Kathleen and Anne were a formative part of my character, and formed an inseparable ring of eccentricity and affection, into which I was often welcomed. They may as well have been like those Stygian witches in Greek mythology, who shared an eyeball and a tooth, because the clucking hens did everything together, were thick as thieves, and for all their formidable intelligence (my goodness they were bright), they loved nothing more than watching Hammer Horror films after a hard day's hawking. The horror film was always accompanied with a packet of smokes and a vat of Guinness.

Aunt Patchy was a font of knowledge, and taught me a lot as I was growing up. Her real name was Sarah, but we called her 'Patchy' because she always had a patch on her dress. She looked like the Hollywood actress Ava Gardner. She had fallen deeply in love as a young nineteen-year-old woman, but her man had sadly died in a car accident. She never fell in love after that, and resigned herself to being single with absolute resolve. When I went out hawking with her, the agreement was that I had to carry the goods, and as we walked from house to house she would explain everything about the trade. 'You're there to carry, listen and you'll learn,' she would tell me. 'Any questions, ask me when I'm on my own or when we're walking home.' I'd ask her a million questions, 'How does that work, Aunt Patchy? Why's that, Aunt Patchy?'

Some days Patchy would wink at me. 'Horror night?' she'd ask.

My dad would see me trooping off to their trailer and say, 'Why are you going to see those clucking hens again, what are they teaching you in there?' And me, I would sit amongst their warm feathers, feasting on biscuits and glasses of milk, between fighting to see the telly through a fog of tobacco, and coughing like hell as they chain-smoked, drank Guinness and told me what was about to happen. They were the best of times.

My favourite actor was Peter Cushing, whether he was playing a good guy like Dr Van Helsing or a sinister villain, he was brilliant in every film that he did. He was also a real family man. Cushing was invited to America by the big studios, and could've been a very big international star but, because his wife was frequently ill, it was more important to him to take care of her, and so he never made the jump over the Atlantic. Instead he settled on the Kent coast, in the hope that the sea air would improve her health. She died in 1971 and he was never the same afterwards; he kept on making films, with the odd notable role like in *Star Wars*, but life just lost its excitement for him. You'll think I'm a train spotter for saying this, but I'm such a fan of his I even went to see Mr Cushing's white wooden house by the sea in Whitstable.

Vampires seem to be in the family. My cousin Jimmy was born with just two teeth in his head, his canine fangs! He's in his sixties now and he's still got those Dracula teeth.

Charles Bronson (the actor, rather than the long-term prisoner who took his name) is also one of my favourite actors. He has a quiet presence that seems to draw you in. Michael Winner, who directed him in the *Death Wish* films once said of him, 'He has great strength on-screen, even when he's standing still or in a completely passive role. There is a depth, a mystery – there is always that sense that something will happen.' As you can imagine, I love the film *Hard Times*, about 'Cheney' (Bronson's character), the backstreet bare-knuckle boxer, who fights his way through the Depression to survive.

The eleventh of fifteen children, Bronson was the son of an illiterate Lithuanian coal miner who died when he was ten. As a kid, Bronson relied on the hand-me-down clothes of his older siblings, and once had to go to school in his sister's dress. He honed that wiry physique not in a gym but through mining from the age of sixteen until he was twenty. The Buchinsky family (his real surname) grew up in a level of poverty most of us can barely imagine, and yet from this terrible start in life he became the highest-paid actor in Hollywood, and the world's favourite star.

Charles Bronson once said, 'I don't have any friends and I don't want any friends.' And I agree. Although I spend a fair bit of time training with Tyson and Tommy, I'm semi-retired. My ideal day is to get my jobs blitzed and out of the way in the morning, then to come back home, knowing I haven't cut any corners, make a cup of tea and watch a Dracula movie or a Bronson action film. I'm not big on company, I have no real friends. It's been like this most of my life, perhaps because – like my dad – I'm suspicious of people. He used to say, 'If you can find one genuine friend that likes you throughout your life, you're doing well.'

Every so-called friend I've ever trusted has let me down in the end. I've lived this side of Cheshire for a long time now, over thirty years, and I've found that it's hard to find like-minded people here. Dracula fans? I shouldn't think there are too many of those around these parts, but you never know, one of these days I may bump into one. Let's just say I'm not holding my breath.

To fit in here you need to drive a flashy car and be obsessed about money. I don't try and tell people how much I'm worth because I find it meaningless and vulgar.

But also because I'm not worth much. That said, the difference between me and a lot of these jumped-up collagen bums is that what I do have, I own. I'm not mortgaged up to my eyes for something I don't need, and nobody is breathing down my back. I'd say that counts for a lot.

I'm very lucky to be able to say I have two of my sons, Shane and John Boy, living close by with their family (actually, they live on either side of my house), while my lad Tommy lives a few miles down the road, not far from Manchester. Tyson lives in Morecambe with his ever-growing clan and I try to see them as much as I can. These days I'll go up perhaps once a fortnight, where I spend time with the grandchildren, go and do jobs for the elderly and keep fit in Tyson's gym.

Ghosts

I believe in ghosts and have one that lives on my farm. Ghosts are like snapshots in time; they do the same thing, following the same patterns that they did in life, only they do it silently on a loop, just like a ghost train is bound by the track it runs on. I don't think they have any freedom in where they go, nor do I think they are sentient, they don't feel anything.

When I was twenty-six I bought a rundown 200-year-old cottage on a large bit of land in Styal, a spit from what's now become the very fashionable Wilmslow, home to umpteen footballers' wives, and a stone's throw from Manchester Airport. It's here that I still live today. Behind the cottage is a large field, which doubtless property developers would love to get their hands on. In front is a yard, part of which is dedicated to the sale of second-hand cars, while the other half is a business my sons run, where people can store their car while they are abroad (obviously for a price!).

There was no running water or electricity for the first years. Here my two lads, John Boy and Tyson, myself and my wife Amber all lived in a caravan, while I gradually did the place up with the help of visiting bricklayers and electricians. I was pretty handy, I suppose, so while the tradesmen did the essential stuff, like rewiring and plumbing, I did the labouring and heavy lifting. A job worth doing is worth doing well and it took ten years to get it completely habitable and to the point we were ready to move in. I had always been brought up to spend what I had, rather than borrow what I hadn't, so it was a bit-by-bit project; I did what I could as and when I had the spare cash.

Now, the people I bought this dilapidated house from were called Gladys and Tommy Harris. They themselves had bought it in the 1940s. Back then it was a two-up and two-down, built in 1805. Tommy was a chimney sweep by trade. He died upstairs. I tracked Gladys down to an old people's home in Gatley, and occasionally I'd go and see her for a cup of tea and a natter. The first time we met

she was in her late seventies, and when I introduced myself
her face lit up and she said, 'I understand you bought the
smallholding.'

'That's right.'

She smiled at me. 'There's a lot of stuff that goes on
there that you're going to have to get your head around.'

'What do you mean?' I asked.

'Do you believe in ghosts?' she asked, a twinkle in her
eye. I suppose she was about seventy-seven, but she was
completely compos mentis, she had all her marbles.

'Well,' I said, 'that depends.'

'Before my husband Tommy and I bought the place, it
was owned by a man called Alfred Cork. In the field next
to the house, he used to cut the wheat with a scythe, all
on his own . . .'

I thought back to a few months after I'd bought the
place, when I was all on my own in the house one night,
tinkering around. I hadn't had the fireplace cleaned out
yet, and I wondered if it was working okay. I got it going
with some kindling and it was working fine. That was a
good sign: Gypsies love nothing more than a good fire.
There was so much to do on the house to make it habitable
and extend it sufficiently for my young and ever-expanding
family. I was just thinking about floorboarding the house
as I reached up to grab some more coal from the shelf
above the hearth, when I caught sight of myself in the
mirror, an old mirror that still hangs on my wall today. My
heart stopped. In the reflection it wasn't just me on my

own in here; I was now in the company of another. His face was so clear that I could tell he was in his sixties, an old man wearing a pork-pie hat, his expression sombre, as if perhaps he wasn't happy with this interloper stood in his front room.

Dumbfounded, for three or four seconds I stood there, looking at the reflection. And when I shot round to look him straight in the eye, there was nobody there. But for the crackle of the flames and a distant hoot from an owl, there were no sounds at all.

There's a lot of stuff that goes on there that you're going to have to get your head around . . . The old dear's words came back to me. 'It was owned by a man called Alfred Cork, and he's never left it.'

Alfred Cork.

A year went by, I was outdoors, doing some work on the interior of the caravan. There was a light on outside and you could see the shadow of anything that passed on the drawn blinds. I had the TV going and, as I glanced at the blind, a shadow of a man appeared and, as clearly etched as a silhouette cutting, it slid across the room. I had a Rottweiler-Doberman cross back then. It was a mean machine, a guard dog par excellence. It was scared of nothing, as you can imagine. But tonight it was silent. I went outside. 'Who goes there?' I said to the darkness.

No answer. Then, in the distance against the twilight, I saw a darker shadow wearing an old mackintosh coat and a hat.

The man must have gone around the back of the shed, I thought to myself, slowly following in his tracks. *So how in hell did the figure walk right past the dog without it going mental?* The alarm bells in my head started going off. I reached the dog's kennel, its chain was gone and the dog had disappeared inside. Inside, the beast was shaking with fear.

I carried on around the back of the shed, but the silent figure had vanished.

A few weeks later, I was chatting with a neighbour who's sadly long since passed, an old fella called Barry Tyler. 'Oh, I could tell you stories about your old farm that would make your toes curl!' He laughed. 'Have you met Alfred yet?'

'Alfred Cork,' I said.

'That's the one.' He smiled. 'He's still about, you know?'

I said, 'I've seen him!'

'Oh yes, doesn't surprise me that. There are so many stories about him being seen up and down here over the years.'

'When did he sell the place?'

'Oh around 1940,' answered Barry.

I shivered, even though it was a warm day. It was 1991; more than forty years had passed and Alfred Cork was still haunting the place.

This next story happened no more than about three months ago. As I was leaving the house with a pal, he suddenly stopped cold. 'Whoah!' he said.

'What's up?' I asked.

'I've just seen this old lady.' He went on to describe Gladys Harris, the previous owner of the house who had told me the story about Alfred Cork. She had stayed in that old people's home in Gatley until her death in 1999. While she was still alive, though, she often walked the two miles from the home back to her beloved old house to check that everything was fine.

'Do you want me to drive you back to the home, Gladys?' I'd ask.

'No, just let me have a look round,' she'd say. Perhaps she had come back to keep her husband Tommy company. This particular day, she'd been stood where the old fireplace used to be before I removed it to extend the walls. I've never seen her ghost myself, though.

Growing up here, my kids certainly had reservations about the house. Cupboards would sometimes open and close of their own accord. My lad Hughie used to say, 'Dad, I don't like this house.'

'Why not?' I'd ask.

'Something's not right here, there's some*one* in my room.'

'There's nobody in your room.'

'Yeah there is, there's somebody in my room.'

Before bed, my son Hughie used to leave his toy Matchbox cars downstairs, all neatly parked together. But in the morning the cars would be in a different place; someone had moved them during the night. As soon as he was of legal age, Hughie moved out to another place and wouldn't come back into the house. They say that children's imaginations are still open, so they are more attuned to the presence of ghosts than adults, but some nights, when I stood in the kids' room after they wouldn't go to sleep because of the noises, I too could hear the faint sound of people talking, almost as if there was a small party going on. Old memories lived on in the masonry of the house, inside its ancient bones.

Why had Alfred Cork been so attached to this place near the banks of the River Bollin? I wondered then, as still I wonder now. Only recently I was out in the yard loading a big Luton van at four in the morning to drive to South Wales a few hours later. I was faffing about with something under the bright electric arc lights, and all of a sudden there was the full shadow of Alfred Cork across the side of the van. Hat and all.

I have even seen my dear old mother here. When I'm really down, she visits me for just a few seconds and then she's gone. She's not the only member of my family who has visited me here at the farm. In 2014 my brother Hughie had an accident while moving a caravan when the draw bar fell and smashed his shin. At first he refused the surgeons' suggestion that they fix his leg with screws and bolts, because he worried about catching an infection through the open skin and it making his type 1 diabetes even worse, Hughie opted instead to have the leg plastered. It was still giving him a lot of pain, though, so he finally agreed to go under the knife and have a metal plate inserted.

Tragically, our dear Hughie suffered a heart attack on the operating table after a clot travelled to his lung. He was in a coma for eleven weeks before he died.

Some time afterwards, I was in the front room with my brother Peter, reminiscing about our big brother and wondering how we would cope without him, such was the vast emptiness his passing had left behind. We were looking at a framed picture of Hughie when, beside us, a four-legged music box that had worked only once, the day I bought it ten years earlier, suddenly came back to life. It played itself without being wound up, for about thirty seconds, and then stopped. I don't doubt for a second that it was powered by Hughie from the afterlife. It's never worked since that day.

There's something about this house, it's like a natural drug to me; the sense of peace I get from being here is irreplaceable. The only way I'll ever leave this place is in a box. Like the others before me, I don't doubt I shall occasionally reappear and walk among the chickens and horses at twilight. I have another house in Salford with Chantal, and in the winter months I spend my time between the farm and hers, but if I am away from the farm for too long, it messes with my head and I have to come back. Come the fair-weather months I live outside there in my caravan. I like the sound of the chickens crowing in the morning and the birds whistling. You can't get that in a row of terraced houses.

A lucky person is one who benefits from a contrast

between the places they live. In many ways I have two lives; the one I lead with a settled person, and the other here on the farm outside in the caravan, which is more of a Gypsy existence. You can't take the Gypsy out of the man, and fortunately for me Chantal understands that; she's always known I'm not a person who can be hemmed in and controlled. The other day the sky was a warm blue, the bees and blossom out and Chantal said, 'Spring's coming, you'll be ready for going soon, John.'

Tyson hit me with a

left hook to the body which

broke three of my ribs.

15

John Fury's Boxing Hall of Fame

Alongside my family and my land, boxing is my true love. It's changed my life and that of my whole family; there's nothing else like it. Now that you know a bit more about me and what makes me tick, I'm hoping you'll indulge me as I tell you a little bit more about the world of boxing, and my favourite fighters and classic fights.

I've always said that 'styles make fights', and I believe that certain boxers bring out the best in other boxers, while other pairings lack that special electricity. These can end up being plodding affairs, where nothing happens and the viewer feels disappointed for making the investment of time and money.

The difference between a good fight and a super fight is that the first delivers two men doing what they are paid to do, going twelve rounds of boxing, or maybe ending in a knockout having shown the audience a fair scrap. Whereas a super fight cannot be predicted; it's like an alignment of the planets. It's one in which one fighter is not hugely better than the other, nor is one at the end of his career and one much younger. It's that rare moment, when two warriors at the apex of their craft and physical prime meet, with all their skills and experience, and each pull from the other the very best that they have within them. A super fight is a meeting of styles, where one fighter's might be very different from the other's, but their talent and their determination to win is equally matched. It's the ultimate Greek tragedy, where only one can be the victor Achilles, who drags his opponent Hector's body around the city walls until it's an unrecognizable mush of blood, cartilage and sand. The other boxer must be vanquished, though his name will for ever be writ large as half of the pair who forged this near mythic scrap. While there are dozens of pairings that deserve to be remembered for ever, only a select few make it into my Hall of Fame.

Top 5 super fights of the modern era

Marvin 'Marvelous' Hagler vs Thomas 'Hitman' Hearns (Caesars Palace, Las Vegas, 15 April 1985)

The first super fight that comes to mind is Marvin 'Marvelous' Hagler versus Thomas 'Hitman' Hearns in

1985. Unlike the Sugar Ray Leonard vs Hagler battle two years later (after which Hagler lost the decision, retired, and never boxed again), at thirty-one, Hagler, the pound-for-pound best middleweight on the planet, still had plenty of juice in the tank and lots of southpaw guile to hurl at Hearns, who was four years his junior. Leonard, no doubt under the wily advice of his coach, Angelo Dundee, waited to come out of retirement and announce his challenge only once Marvin had slowed down and passed his peak. That was still an amazing fight, also at Caesars Palace, and one in which Ray Leonard claimed, 'It was the closest I've been to death,' but it is not comparable to when Hagler fought Hearns in April 1985. This was billed as 'The Fight' but, given the ferocity of the toe-to-toe three rounds that followed, it was aptly rechristened 'The War'. There was none of the usual time spent feeling each other out for the first few rounds, when fighters find their reach and gradually settle down into exchanging bigger, riskier shots and combinations. Instead, Hagler and Hearns flew out of their corners like whirling dervishes on a mission to knock each other out in the first round, with scant regard for tiring themselves out; it's a testament to the amazing physical condition they were in that they were able to keep this pace going.

Hagler's answer to Hearns's three-inch reach advantage was to take the fight to the other's body. The continuous exchanges of fists still make you wince as you watch that fight, as both sides give no quarter. Hearns fired eighty-three punches, landing fifty-four, while Hagler threw fifty of eighty-two. That's a staggering work rate. At this pace the fight couldn't last for long; surely one of them would have to capitulate to the other.

Nine seconds before the end of the first round, Hagler caught Hearns with a straight right sending him reeling backwards, but rather than trying to get away from Hagler in the closing seconds before the bell, the Hitman bravely flew straight back at him with a volley of punches. No wonder, looking back on his illustrious career, Marvellous Marvin would say this fight was the peak moment of his career. This was his eleventh defence of his title. The only man with a chin sufficiently tough enough to take him the whole fifteen rounds was Roberto Durán.

As the bell sounded to end the first round and the warriors returned to their respective corners, the vicious first three minutes had already taken a brutal toll on both of them; Hagler was badly cut under his right eye, while Hearns's right hand was broken (weakened by a previous injury, it had cracked as the Hitman delivered an uppercut to Hagler's iron chin). Hagler, ever vigilant of his prey, realized what had happened as he felt the reduced power of Hearns's right fist, and wasted no time in switching stance to orthodox to outfox his opponent, who by now was reduced to an unconvincing but persistent right-hand jab. However, the odds were evened by an ugly gash Hearns had inflicted above Hagler's eye in round one – if Tommy Hearns could just keep out of trouble and pepper a few more shots to the injury, the bout might well be stopped and be classed as a TKO (technical knockout) in Hearns's favour.

The third round saw a watchful referee separating the men from getting into clinches, which spoiled Hagler boxing on the inside, allowing Hearns to fire from a distance and use his superior reach. Hagler was getting pissed off by the delays keeping him from taking care of business. And so a minute and a half into the third, when the referee stopped the fight so a ringside doctor could check on Hagler's eye and asked him if he could see, a furious Hagler hissed, 'I'm still hitting him, aint I?' As he later said, 'I had to get serious and get it done quickly.'

The boy from Newark with the polished bald head and face of an enraged demon finally stamped his authority on the challenger from Motor City with a right that almost spun Hearns around, following it with a right hook to the temple and a powerful shot to the jaw. As Hearns rose on wobbly legs to the count of nine, the referee, Richard Steele, stopped the fight.

Fury vs Wilder 3 'Once and For All' (T-Mobile Arena, Nevada, USA, 9 October 2021)

It's difficult not to get emotional thinking about this fight when I consider the terrible things that were happening in the months that preceded it. If you look at the post-fight moments in the ring again, you'll see Tyson leaning on the ropes with his brother Shane, saying a prayer of gratitude. What viewers didn't know was that in the run-up to their third clash, Tyson had far bigger fish to fry than Wilder, which meant he'd barely had three-and-a-half weeks in training camp in preparation for the fight. He also needed surgery for an injury. All this on top of the fact Tyson had contracted Covid in July, which forced him to delay the fight.

The following month, and still during the pandemic, Paris had given birth to their sixth child, a baby girl called Athena. Doctors were alarmed that her heart was beating twice as rapidly as it should have been, and she was rushed from the Royal Lancaster Infirmary where she was born, and placed in an intensive care unit at Alder Hey Children's Hospital in Liverpool. Poor Athena was in an incubator with a tube down her throat to help her breathe, given sedatives to help her sleep, painkillers, and beta blockers for heart. Paris was holding her when suddenly she felt her heartbeat fading away and she stopped breathing completely. She flatlined and was officially dead for three minutes.

Unlike that night in my prison cell, when I had the vision of Jesus by my bed telling me that Tyson's little boy Prince would be fine, fortunately, this time I was here in the flesh with Tyson. But I could offer little solace; his spirits couldn't have been any lower. Mercifully, his daughter made a full recovery. But to go from a triple whammy of illness, injury and life-threatening family trauma, and only a few weeks later do what Tyson did to

Wilder, was like moving mountains. Somehow my son dug deep, spoke to his Lord, and produced one half of one of the best fights this century has witnessed.

Fury vs Wilder 3 was so packed with drama it was exhausting to watch! Right from the bell, it was epic in scale; there was drama, with both men making multiple visits to the canvas, and there was heart and skill. There was also history between the two fighters that added something special. The third meeting of these two titans was, from a boxing fan's perspective, the best of the three encounters between the Gypsy King and the Bronze Bomber. From a father's perspective, they are all special and unforgettable. As I've been quoted as saying rather indelicately, Tyson comes from my ball bag (!) and to think that I partly produced a talent like that . . . I still have to pinch myself sometimes.

After being dominated in their second fight, Wilder had gone away to assess his weaknesses. His regroup certainly paid dividends; he returned on 9 October a humbler man with a very determined mindset – he was prepared to do anything to win back his WBC belt. He'd worked to great effect on combinations with his new trainer, Malik Scott, and had become a more three-dimensional fighter, not just reliant on his killer right bomb, which throughout his career had helped him with the consistency of Thor's hammer. However, while Wilder had done plenty of preparation and was hungrier than ever, Tyson, through no fault of his own, was not at his best.

Tyson had sparred excessively in training, ten and twelve rounds. His coach SugarHill should have known better than that. You don't need that amount of sparring; it's like having two twelve-round fights in one week. Even with headgear on and big gloves, you've still got huge men swinging at you, and your body is constantly taking stick. That level of contact takes the edge off you and in the long-term it knocks hell out of your brain.

Despite my private reservations about his training preparation, I assured Tyson that he'd had a good camp and had done enough. As a father, all you can do is try and get your son in the right headspace; I knew he was only 50 per cent fit, that his mind was on other things, and that having had twenty months out of the ring, he was completely rusty. I was worried that he was trying to please other people at his own cost. I said, 'You're not physically ready for this. Delay it. You'll probably get loads of flak, but isn't it better to do the job properly?'

'I can't pull out,' he said, 'I have to go in injured. I've done it before and I'll do it again. People are depending on me, I don't want to let them down. The lads in the trenches at the Somme and Ypres didn't have a choice, they had to go over the top.' Ever the historian!

So, having tried to talk him out of it, I was now just trying to be positive. I thought, *It will take an extraordinary individual to turn this around but then again, if anybody is extraordinary that has to be Tyson. You've always defied the odds and been full of surprises.*

It took me back to when Tyson was fourteen years old. He was sparring with his younger brother Shane all over the house, and I told them, 'I'm sick of you smashing the place up, take it outside.' I followed them out and said, 'Okay, let's see what you're made of. I want you to punch me on the body as hard as you can, and if you're any good you can start training properly with other boxers in the gym.'

Tyson hit me with a left hook to the body which broke three of my ribs. *This kid can do anything.*

Fast-forward to October 2021 and, as the two fighters touched gloves, Tyson had a savage, unpredictable look in his eyes, filled with venom. I knew Hell was coming for breakfast. My lad knew he wasn't fit enough to dance for twelve rounds, and he was prepared to fight a slugfest rather than a masterclass.

At the sound of the first bell, both fighters flew out their corners for possession of the centre of the ring, Wilder showing noticeably improved footwork as he got down to business jabbing at Tyson's body. The Bronze Bomber seemed fresh and confident, mixing plenty of head and body shots and pressing Tyson onto the back foot. The first round ended with a great right from Tyson.

Round two saw him beginning to relax, counterpunching well while also absorbing some straight jabs to the body. Come round three, Tyson had landed nineteen to Wilder's thirteen; however, the Bronze Bomber was looking very dangerous, throwing and connecting with some great left hooks and his infamous rights. My hope was that Wilder would start to forget all the things he'd worked on, and return to throwing right bombs. So far that hadn't happened.

Tyson's right-hand shots made deafening cracks as he hit the sweet spot again and again. The referee took him aside and warned him about clinches and holding Wilder in a headlock. Thirty seconds before the end of round three, Tyson hit him with a magic right uppercut and Wilder collapsed like one of Fred Dibnah's felled cooling chimneys. Timber-r-r-r! Wilder had said he was prepared to go out on his shield in true Spartan style, and clearly he meant it. He was up on his pins and saved by the bell.

Come round four, Tyson was patiently looking for an opportunity to knock his opponent out, while Deontay's legs looked shaky as jelly. He unleashed a flurry of punches with Wilder on the ropes but suddenly, out of nowhere, the Bomber's lethal hammer appeared and dropped Tyson on the canvas with an overhead. Tyson was up on his feet with thirty-five seconds remaining in the round. Wilder pressed home his advantage and knocked Tyson down for a *second* time; you could hear the slap of bone on canvas reverberating around the stadium. Once again, Tyson was back on his feet and saved by the bell. For Wilder to have been knocked down and come back in the next round to knock Tyson out not only once but twice, was pure testament to how much he wanted his title back.

Tyson was fast becoming the bout's power puncher. In the fifth, Tyson, visibly furious at being knocked down in the last round, flew out of his corner like a bloody Viking berserker. In contrast, Wilder seemed unusually chilled. He was woken up with a right hand that made him shake. Wilder responded with a cracking strong right, but for the most part of that round, both fighters were ginger with their punches as they both sought to recover and regain some kind of equilibrium. They were both still finding their form when the bell went.

Commentators between the fifth and sixth round were already designating this a very special fight and one in which, for a change, Wilder had come with a plan and was sticking to it like Bostik. But by the time the sixth round began, Wilder was beginning to look a little weary on his feet, with Tyson tying him up in clinches, and he soon wobbled and took the knee. With two minutes to go, the Gypsy King had landed sixty-two punches to Wilder's thirty-four, though worryingly, some unofficial scorecards had Wilder ahead by two points with forty-seven to Tyson's forty-five.

By the seventh round, it had become a war of attrition straight out of a movie; like the last round of *Rocky* with Apollo Creed trading punch for punch with the Italian stallion. Just when it looked like victory was in Tyson's crosshairs, Wilder would respond with amazing valour, keeping himself in the race and doggedly refusing to give up. Maybe it was that Malik Scott had just screamed at him to 'wake the fuck up!' in the corner, but something supernatural seemed to be keeping him going. Tyson worked at the Bronze Bomber's body relentlessly, hitting him with a beautiful overhead right. Wilder was swinging wildly and punching thin air, Tyson had him pinned down in the corner, where he connected a textbook uppercut that *should* have been the end of his foe. Even George Foreman would've been destroyed by that shot.

In the eighth round, Tyson was hunting Wilder down and the other was walking into his shots. An unofficial scorecard had them both tagged at sixty-seven points. With a minute remaining, both fighters' legs were weary. In the next round, Tyson caught Wilder with a stiff jab. He'd landed 120 shots to Wilder's sixty-one and was stepping things up. Big right hands and one-twos were what Tyson dished out at the start of the tenth. With just under a minute and a half left, Wilder threw a left hook which Tyson neatly ducked and counterpunched, knocking Wilder down with a mighty right hook. Tyson came in for the kill, but at the end of the round Wilder found the last shred of energy and finished the attack.

In the end it came down to the better fighter winning, as Tyson pummelled Deontay Wilder into submission, culling him with a two-shot. The battle royal was over. Both fighters had walked the talk and given their everything.

From a boxing perspective, style went out the window for the third and final part of the Fury-Wilder trilogy. It was not a display of finesse, nor was it an exhibition of the sweet science. Instead it was an ugly war in which my son stood toe-to-toe with a man whose right-hand punch could fairly lay claim to being as powerful as that of Mike Tyson and George Foreman. For the paying public, it turned out to be the equivalent of watching two gladiators in the Colosseum, with plenty of blood, courage and excitement. But given that Tyson is an exemplary boxer, a craftsman of his trade, it was painful to watch him absorb those right bombs knowing that the usual Tyson would've moved out of the way. He wasn't fit enough to be slick, and instead walked onto Wilder's right hand in the fourth round like a rookie. Down he went.

After the fight Tyson told me, 'I couldn't box, couldn't work my jab. Every time I threw a jab the pain was unbearable. So I was boxing two people in there – pain in my body, and him. All we could do was make a war of it and I wanted to win more than he did. Either he gets me or I get him. Trench warfare. After he knocked me down in the fourth round I thought, *here we go, dogfight mode.*'

One thing I know about my son is that – unless Tyson is out of his senses – he'll get up and never let the ref count him out, that's the way of the warrior. As Larry Holmes said many years ago, 'It takes a world-class fighter to climb up off the floor and win.' And Tyson is nothing if not that. He's a veteran of his sport, a natural fighter, and he's been down plenty of times before and got back up.

But a boxer can only take so many punches before those blows start to demand their pound of flesh and take their effect; they are after all knocking the brain around within its skull casing, and it can take just a light jab to break the camel's back. Watching Wilder erode my son's athletic vitality was horrible to witness. There is a saying that you leave a bit of yourself in the ring with every fight. I wonder how much it cost Tyson to retain his crown.

Ali vs Foreman 'The Rumble in the Jungle' (Kinshasa, Zaire, 30 October 1974)

This wasn't just any old fight. It took place in the heart of Africa, in the capital city of Zaire (now known as the Democratic Republic of Congo). The country's leader, President Mobutu, in an attempt to put the country on the map, had offered what was then an extraordinary $10 million to bring the fight to Kinshasa. With such a grand investment, he left little to chance in terms of bad PR, allegedly rounding up 1,000 of Kinshasa's leading criminals before the fight and the arrival of the world's press, holding them in rooms under the stadium before executing 100 of them to make his point; if anyone stepped out of line or so much as thought about criminal activity in the country during the fight, they knew exactly what would happen to them. Unsurprisingly, the city was free of crime for the event. The country was still recovering from years of colonialism and political instability, but tonight, the world's attention was focused on this small corner of the continent.

It's hard to think of a super fight with as many of the magic ingredients that the Rumble in the Jungle involved.

There is fear, despair, courage and impending tragedy. The two lead actors couldn't have been more different. First, enter the Minotaur, George Foreman. Not since Sonny Liston had the heavyweight division seen a bullish fighter who inspired such fear. Perhaps it was because of the way Foreman took his opponents apart – he didn't just dismantle them, he mercilessly stripped them of their masculinity. He was a relentless clubbing machine who had walked through the rock-hard punches of Ali's nemesis, Joe Frazier, when the latter defended his title in Jamaica at what was billed as the Sunshine Showdown in 1973. Foreman made Joe's best shots look as if he was being hit by wet paper bags. But it was the magnitude of Foreman's punches that was most disturbing, as he sent Frazier flying around the ring. Even the indomitable Joe Frazier had no strategy to beat him! Foreman knocked him out in just a minute and a half, taking his title in the process.

Enter the challenger. Ali, the self-proclaimed 'Greatest of All Time', was very much the underdog; seven years older than George Foreman, he'd previously lost to Joe Frazier and Ken Norton, both of whom Foreman had swatted effortlessly out of the way. But Ali, always bigger than boxing, began to connect with the people as soon as he set foot in Zaire. He seemed to have colluded with a local witch doctor, and was working his dark sorcery over the brutish, introverted Foreman too. Ali was determined to convince himself and everybody else that he was going to whup George Foreman. *'Ali boma ye!'* he sang (the

Congolese for 'Ali 's going to kill him!') to everyone, and it became a kind of rhythmic mantra that the crowd started singing with him. A testament to his ability to hold audiences spellbound, Ali had charmed a nation.

Ali was not a knockout merchant; rather he was a master of movement and strategy, known for his quick footwork, his ability to outmanoeuvre opponents and, of course, his lightning-fast jabs. But George Foreman seemed invincible and many thought that Ali's mercurial punches would be as threatening as a wasp flying around a giant. You only have to watch *When We Were Kings*, a brilliant documentary about the fight, to see the damage that Foreman inflicted on the heavy bag in preparation with his fists, leaving huge dents in their wake. Foreman is still considered the boxer with the heaviest, most formidable fist power ever.

It was a cold evening in Cheshire where I sat waiting at a friend's house for the big fight to start, but thousands of miles away, it was a humid night in Kinshasa, Zaire, the air thick with anticipation. The world had been waiting for this moment for months, and there'd been a delay because Foreman had sustained an injury in training. Both fighters were ordered to remain in the tiny African country while Foreman healed. The fight was set to take place in the early hours of 30 October 1974, and the entire world was watching.

As the fighters made their way to the ring, the 65,000 fans in the stadium roared with excitement. Ali had hatched a plan that he believed would bring him victory. He was not nearly as strong as his opponent, and it would've been suicide had he tried to take him on toe-to-toe like Norton and Frazier. Ali, ever the intelligent Theseus, worked out another way that he could beat the Minotaur, and for months before the fight had been conditioning his body to withstand heavy punches, his sparring partners constantly firing shots to his stomach.

As the bell rang for the first round, the two fighters approached each other warily and Ali danced around the ring, taunting Foreman and dodging his punches. The crowd was on their feet, cheering Ali on with 'Ali boma ye'. But Foreman wasn't deterred, he continued to press forward, closing off the ring. Ali danced and taunted, landing solid hits. Foreman was all business, trying to land a knockout blow. And then, in the second round, he caught Ali with a powerful punch that sent him to the mat. I remember thinking, *This is curtains, Ali's done for.*

But Ali got back up, and kept fighting.

As the fight wore on, Ali's strategy soon became clear; he was using a technique he'd developed called the 'rope-a-dope', in which he would lean back against the ropes, allowing Foreman to pummel him while blocking, and though it looked like he was absorbing all of the punishment from those punches, many of them were absorbed not by his body, but his arms, then transferred into the ropes. Ali was conserving his energy.

Foreman grew frustrated. He couldn't land a knockout

blow on Ali, and he was starting to tire. Ali, on the other hand, seemed to be gaining strength as the fight went on. He continued to taunt Foreman up close with, 'Come on George, that all you got?', bull hammering him as if he was just another heavy bag. Now Ali was landing more and more punches on Foreman.

Ali looked like he was playing with him as he danced into a corner, settling down for another round of rope-a-dope, and then suddenly launching a devastating display of counterpunching, with volleys of jabs and lightning-quick hooks. This went on round after round, until they reached the eighth, and Ali saw his opportunity. He unleashed a flurry of punches on Foreman, and the champion staggered. Ali continued to land blow after blow, and Foreman was unable to defend himself. Finally, the great bull collapsed to the canvas, the entire continent of Africa shaking with the impact, and the referee counted him out.

It was a stunning upset, and it cemented Ali's status as one of the greatest boxers of all time. But it was more than just a boxing match. It was a battle of wills, a clash of styles, and a moment in history that will never be forgotten. Norman Mailer, the renowned writer and journalist, was there to witness the Rumble in the Jungle first hand. He described the fight as a 'titanic struggle', and he marvelled at Ali's ability to absorb punishment and come back stronger. In his book, *The Fight*, Mailer wrote: 'The Rumble in the Jungle was more than just a boxing match, it was a test of character, a battle of wills. Ali and Foreman were two of the greatest fighters of their time, and they brought everything they had to the ring that night. But it was Ali who emerged victorious, and he did it with style and grace. He showed us what it means to be a champion, not just in the ring, but in life.'

Now, some people might say that Ali won because Foreman was tired, or because he had underestimated his opponent. But let me tell you, that's not true. Ali won because he was the better fighter, plain and simple. He had a strategy, he executed it perfectly, and he came out on top. The Rumble in the Jungle was a fight for the ages. It was a moment of triumph for Ali, a moment of defeat for Foreman, and a moment of inspiration for millions of people around the world. It was a reminder that anything is possible, that the underdog can triumph, and that sometimes, the greatest battles are fought not with fists, but with heart and guile.

Ali vs Frazier 'The Thrilla in Manila' (Araneta Coliseum, Quezon City, Philippines, 1 October 1975)

The hostility was there, the opposing styles, the shared history of two fights, with one win per fighter. It was a rivalry that would produce one of the most brutal and punishing fights ever, it would take so much from each fighter that they would never be quite the same again. The best fights represent so much more than two men meeting in a roped enclosure and beating hell out of each other;

they reflect the tone of the times and the conflicts within or between nations; in this case the civil rights movement and the ongoing war in Southeast Asia. Their first clash dubbed the 'Fight of the Century' (1971) had more than lived up to its hype, with an unbeaten Ali returning from a four-year ban for refusing to be drafted for Vietnam, versus the WBA, WBC, and the Ring heavyweight champion Joe Frazier. Just to add another exotic layer, both were former Olympians.

Ali was the darling of African Americans and an outspoken exponent of the counterculture; his anti-establishment views and politically dangerous allegiances, like those with Malcolm X and Martin Luther King, created fear and distrust from 'white America'. Because he refused to go to Vietnam to fight for his country, Ali was banned from boxing for three years and thereby robbed of his prime years as a heavyweight. Meanwhile Joe Frazier openly supported the war in Vietnam and found himself being championed by the people who hated his opponent. Something seismic was happening, a volcano building with heat and lava. This was no longer a boxing match; it had become a fight between civil rights reform and the old establishment of America.

Ali was a master of trash-talk and had got under Frazier's skin so deeply that before the first clash, Frazier was praying to God to help him *kill* his opponent. Come the night of 28 March 1971, the very cream of Hollywood glamour was at ringside, from Burt Lancaster to Frank Sinatra to Diana

Ross. Staged at Madison Square Garden, it may still be the most anticipated sporting event ever.

Ali dominated the first five rounds using Frazier's face as a target for his precision jabs. By the sixth Frazier's mug was a mess of welts. But still 'Smokin' Joe' was relentless. By the eleventh round Ali was visibly tiring, and Frazier found a left hook to his jaw that brought Ali down to his gloves on the canvas and a knee. He took another hiding later in the round and barely made it back to his corner.

In the fifteenth, Frazier was ahead on the score cards and put Ali down again and he made the count. While Ali had the skill and reflexes to handle Frazier's erratic ducking and weaving, his own defence had not been active enough to keep the smaller man at bay in this fight. Frazier clinched a fifteen-round victory by points.

By the time they met for their second clash, dubbed 'Superfight II', again at Madison Square Garden in New York, the rivalry and distaste they felt for one another was like a building hurricane; in the build-up they had a real scrap on a live TV talk show. There were no titles at stake as Frazier had lost his crown to George Foreman, and the fight generally lacked the pace and drama of Frazier vs Ali 1. Ali began a predictable pattern of stopping Frazier from boxing on the inside by holding his neck down, then spraying him clusters of shots before repeating the exercise; it was functional but ultimately robbed the fight of its edge. Ali won this twelve-round fight on points, which set the stage for The Thrilla in Manila, which would happen a year later.

Ali enraged Frazier with his street poetry, 'It'll be a killa, and a thrilla and chilla, when I get the gorilla in Manila.' Frazier's response was, 'I despise Ali for trying to misrepresent me to the public; no one gave his heart and soul to the sport as I did. This was a nasty, envious mean-spirited egomaniac, who still couldn't stand the fact that in the biggest fight of his life I'd put him on his ass.' Frazier never fully forgave Ali for some of the comments he made before this fight. The champ could be just as merciless with his verbal shots as his physical ones.

So on that October morning, in unbearable 120°F heat, the two men squared up to one another and touched gloves for what was to be less of a boxing exhibition displaying craft and guile, and more of a pugilistic scrap where the rivals fought toe-to-toe like street-fighters. Both left the ring with their dignity intact, but forever damaged by the Agincourt of shots fired and landed on each other. Boxing pundits, looking back on this fight forty years later, would say: '*The Thrilla in Manila* was the closest to sanctioned manslaughter boxing had allowed since 187lb Jack Dempsey demolished the 6ft 6in champion Jess Willard in three rounds on 4 July, 1919.'

There was no dancing from the new heavyweight champ; in this fight Ali stood firmly in the centre of the ring with his legs planted wide, taking on the fury of Joe Frazier, soaking up vicious hooks and throwing out heavy shots of his own. Frazier seemed to absorb Ali's punches with supernatural tenacity. After the sixth round, Ali was so exhausted he sat down for the first time in his corner. For the next couple of rounds Frazier was boxing close, delivering body hooks and uppercuts, until the twelfth when the tide turned again. Ali pushed back Frazier with a succession of punches that almost closed his left eye with swelling. In the thirteenth round both men were staggering around; it was almost a question of who was going to die first. With two rounds remaining and each boxer fighting on empty, Ali unleashed a volley of punches, nine successive rights to Frazier's head.

Before the bell rang for the fifteenth and final round, Frazier's coach Eddie Futch told his valiant prodigy, 'Joe, I'm going to stop the fight.'

'No, no Eddie, you can't do that to me,' replied Frazier.

'You couldn't see in the last two rounds,' said Futch, 'what makes you think you're going to see in the fifteenth?'

'I want him, boss,' said Frazier, trying to stand up.

'Sit down, son, it's all over. No one will forget what you did here today.'

He was right, the fight has lived on in savage glory long after both boxers handed their gloves to St Peter and passed through the Pearly Gates.

Durán vs Barkley (Convention Hall, Atlantic City, USA, 24 February 1989)

The fight between Roberto Durán and Iran Barkley was a highly anticipated mash-up. Durán, known as 'Hands of Stone', was a former world champion in three weight classes, while Barkley was the reigning middleweight champion. He was fresh off the back of beating Thomas Hearns, while the ageing Durán had taken nineteen months out of the sport having been destroyed by the Hitman (Hearns) in the second round. That made Durán the definitive underdog.

The biggest threat to Durán was himself. He had been in party mode when he should've been in preparation for Hearns. But when Durán was finely conditioned and focused there were none that could match him. For his appointment with Barkley, Durán was in great shape and the fight took place on 24 February 1989 at the Convention Hall in Atlantic City, New Jersey. Seven thousand people turned up for the fight, but they had to brave blizzards in order to get there.

Leading up to the fight, there was a lot of trash-talk between the two fighters. Barkley, who was known for his power and aggressive style, had been calling out Durán for months, claiming that the Panamanian was afraid to fight him. Durán, who was thirty-seven years old at the time, was seen as past his prime, and many believed Barkley would win the fight easily. However, Durán was one of the most fearless men to ever step into a ring. He'd narrowly lost to Hagler, so what was there to be terrified about now? His only nemesis was time; he wasn't getting any younger. Determined to prove that he still possessed a champion's fire in his belly, he trained hard for the fight and focused on his strategy of using superior boxing skills to outmanoeuvre the younger Barkley; Durán was a master of working on the inside, toe-to-toe.

Round one saw Barkley coming out strong, throwing powerful punches and trying to overwhelm Durán with his aggression. He was six inches taller than the Panamanian, with a reach that was seven inches longer. However, Durán was able to avoid most of Barkley's punches and counter with his own shots, landing several hard punches to Barkley's head and body. Just before the bell, Durán landed a brilliant right-hander that shook the champion, but there wasn't sufficient time left to build on this and weaken him further. As the fight progressed, Durán's strategy began to pay off. He was able to use his footwork and defensive skills to thwart Barkley, who was becoming increasingly tired and frustrated. Durán continued to land hard punches on Barkley, who was unable to mount a sustained attack.

The fifth and six rounds were busy, with a quick pace and some great right hands from Durán. In the eighth Barkley threw a huge left hook which connected and wobbled Durán. In the ninth round Durán smiled darkly at the champ, having made the other miss five shots in a row, then responding with a killer left hook.

In the eleventh round, Durán landed a devastating left hook amidst several right crosses, which sent Barkley crashing to the canvas. Barkley was able to get back up, but he was clearly hurt and disoriented. Durán continued to press the attack, landing several more hard punches that left Barkley reeling. Finally, in the twelfth round, Durán landed a vicious left hook that sent Barkley hurtling to the canvas for the second time. The referee stopped the fight, giving Durán a TKO victory and the middleweight championship.

The fight remains a classic in boxing history and is remembered as one of the greatest upsets of all time. It was a testament to Durán's toughness and determination, that, despite being considered past his prime, he was able to rise to the occasion and defeat one of the best middleweight fighters of his era. The victory cemented Durán's legacy as one of the greatest boxers ever, and one of the elite few to have held world titles at four different weight divisions.

My all-time favourite boxers

What is it that makes a great boxer? Is it a big heart, skill, a fast pair of hands and feet that can dance? Or an iron will to prevail, the endurance to fight on with a broken hand (as many have done, from Hearns to Calzaghe) and never give up until they take you out on your shield? Or is it guile and ring smarts, or perhaps a fighter's ability to psyche another out, or grind them down round by round? I don't honestly know, but when I think about the boxers whose fights I go back to watch again and again, and which excite me every time, I would certainly say it's a mix of all these qualities.

Marvin Hagler

To my reckoning, Marvin Hagler was the best middleweight of *all* time. He had an iron chin, balls of steel, extreme determination, and he was a naturally dominant fighter. He was great at setting up shots, he knew the angles and was an awkward southpaw to fight. 'Marvelous Marvin' had all the tools, talent, and the heart to match. He was the unquestioned regent of the ring, and it belonged to him in every fight, up until his very last against Sugar Ray Leonard when the judges' split decision went to Leonard, rankling him to the point that he left the sport for good. He also headed off to Italy to find his way into movies and became an articulate and knowledgeable expert on the sweet science, making for an engaging boxing pundit.

Hagler grew up in the rough streets of Newark, New York, without a father. At thirteen his mother moved the family to Massachusetts because of the race riots. They lived in the town of Brockton, where Rocky Marciano was born, and it was here, at fourteen years of age, that Marvin visited the Petronelli Brothers' Gym. It was in this place that he would hone his fearsome craft; his relationship of trust with the two brothers, Pat and Goody, who became his trainers and managers, would endure for what would become a long and glorious career. Sometimes the best propellant a boxer needs is a coach who steps into the shoes of the father they never had.

But the journey to the top for Marvin was never going

to be straightforward. He lost his first couple of fights to William Monroe and Bobby Watts, and this made it difficult for him to claim the right for a shot at the middleweight title. He had to go back to the drawing board, biding his time until he had both boxers beaten. In 1971 he took on the reigning middleweight champion, Vito Antuofermo, which ended in a draw. After Alan Minter took the crown, he invited Hagler to have another shot at the title in 1980. Hagler went to work with ferocious intent. By the third round Minter's face was a mass of cuts and bruises, and he was clearly no match for the American. The referee stopped the fight, to the fury of the Wembley crowd, who began throwing bottles at the new middleweight champion of the world. Hagler had to shield himself behind his team in the corner of the ring before being escorted to his dressing room.

The fight against Minter was the first time I saw him on TV. He would go on to beat the former champion decisively in a rematch and would successfully defend his title twelve times. Hagler was not stupid, and knew when to quit. On the subject of retirement he reflected, 'Why do you want to hang around after all your hard work and let somebody get lucky and destroy your record? After I had nothing to prove to myself, it was the best thing to walk away.'

Hagler is my favourite middleweight. The man had everything a true fighter needs: heart, skill, determination and bravery. You name it, he had bucketloads of it.

Unlike the next boxer on our list, Marvin kept his team very small; just his promoter, trainer, and his wife managing all his money affairs.

Roberto Durán

Roberto Durán is one of only two boxers – the other being Jack Johnson – to have competed over five decades with a career that spanned from 1968 to 2001. 'Manos de Piedra' (meaning 'hands of stone') was his ominous nom de guerre, as boxers feared the power of his fists and their bone-shaking effect. He has consistently been voted in the top ten boxers of all time by aficionados. In 2002 The Ring magazine voted him 'the fifth greatest fighter for the last eighty years', the Associated Press voted him 'number one lightweight of the twentieth century', while boxing historian Bert Sugar considered him 'the eighth greatest fighter of all time'.

Durán won world championships in four different weight classes: lightweight, welterweight, light middleweight, and middleweight. He also reigns as the undisputed and lineal lightweight champion, and the lineal welterweight champion, no small feat of achievement. In 1972 he scored a thirteen-round knockout of the reigning WBA lightweight champion, Scotsman Ken Buchanan.

Durán was born in El Chorillo, a flyblown slum by the Panama Canal. One of nine children, extreme poverty forced him to steal fruit to help feed his brothers and sisters, and he ran with a group of street urchins constantly in trouble with the law. The legends that surround him are as unbelievable as his real-life achievements, and some just beggar belief. Like the night he was attacked by three men, responding by knocking all of them out. He was only fourteen. They all were arrested and ended up in the same cell! It was a busy year for him, at fourteen he's also remembered as knocking a mule out with one punch.

Durán was famously generous, giving millions to the slums of El Chorillo. He was also a social animal, and would throw lavish parties of epic proportions to which everyone was invited; and that included the street urchins he'd struggled alongside. Long before Iron Mike had a pet tiger, Durán kept Manny, a pet lion.

He first began sparring at the age of eight, making his professional debut in 1968 at the age of sixteen. Durán was all but invincible as a lightweight, and gave up his belts to switch up to a heavier weight and fight at welterweight. It's amazing to think that in sixty-four fights he was only beaten once as a lightweight, by Esteban de Jesús. His first fight against Sugar Ray Leonard was in Montreal in 1980, the same venue where only four years earlier Leonard had produced a gold at the Montreal Olympics.

Classic Durán from the start, he was on the front foot, hunting down his opponent, ducking and weaving. With his pitch-black eyes, shining mane of hair and goatee beard, there was something wolf-like about him; it was as if he belonged in the ring. Throughout his career, a permanent anger radiated from his body that could only be exorcized by the priests of his stone fists against another man's bones. In the fight against Ray Leonard, his punishment of the other was unremitting, and Ray, even if he was the most talented boxer in the world at the time, got dragged into a street fight in which he was completely out of his depth. You see Durán was a master of boxing on the inside, toe-to-toe, close up, and if you were daft enough to get drawn into a clinch, he would make short work of you.

The 'Brawl in Montreal' as the fight became known, was regarded by many as Durán's supreme moment (in truth Durán had many supreme moments), as the Panamanian took Leonard to the cleaners in fifteen brilliant rounds of boxing, winning clearly in a unanimous points decision. In dethroning the king and winning his WBC belt, Durán also became world champion in a second weight class. Roberto had questioned Leonard's manhood and severely dented his confidence.

Just as Ricky Hatton allowed his waistline to balloon between fights, but got back in terrific shape for the next battle, Durán would increasingly struggle to keep his weight down. It wasn't just food that he was excessive with; after each fight he would lose himself in a hedonistic blur of alcohol and women – and this party might last for months – before having to clean up, slim down and earn some more money for his next fight. And it was this easily identifiable cycle that Ray Leonard and his coach Angelo Dundee exploited when, thoroughly haunted and depressed by his defeat in Montreal, Leonard demanded an instant rematch in late November of the same year. He knew Durán was still in full-throttle party mode, the likes of which would've left the Happy Mondays in pieces, and that the scheduling of the suggested rematch allowed little time to get fit.

Durán was ever the split personality between excess and discipline, not to mention that hosting the world's best party demands cash, so, reluctantly he agreed, and went to work to shed the extra pounds from his bloated body in the limited time he had available. It seemed the *'no mas'* fight was doomed before it even started.

On the night of 25 November, the legendary boxer left Panama for New Orleans as a shadow of his former self; slightly overweight and far from fit. He felt he'd been prematurely uprooted from his festivities. In contrast it was a very different Leonard who presented himself this time around. Ray Leonard seemed to be working to two basic principles: the first being to avoid getting into any street-fighter clinches, the second being to rile and humiliate his opponent as much as possible; get him so mad he would blow himself out. He certainly achieved that; from the first bell, Leonard danced around the ring taunting Durán with his showboating feints and fancy footwork.

Durán had eaten two steaks before the fight, felt sluggish, and was complaining of a stomach upset. He didn't have the energy or the inclination to chase after Leonard. Compared to the pace with which he'd closed the ring off in Montreal, he now looked decidedly lacklustre. His campaign to nail Leonard down in the corner dissolved from attempted clusters into single shots, and he was tired and gasping for air like a guppy fish by the end of the first.

By the time the seventh round arrived, Leonard's inner trickster was on full display; sticking his chin out for Durán to try and hit, 'Ali shuffling' then, the ultimate insult, faking a bolo punch with his right, then throwing a straight right jab into Durán's face. In the eighth round, with just thirty seconds remaining, Durán put his hand up, turned his back on his opponent and walked off to his corner, thereby committing the ultimate sin in boxing; he had given up, quit. Pound for pound the world's most feared pugilist – the man who was afraid of nothing and no one, the man-child who'd knocked out three fully-grown men at the age of fourteen, who had owned his own pet lion – had quit. The sports world would shortly reel off its axis, as if one of the planets had dropped out of the sky.

Durán is alleged to have said '*no mas*', *no more*, but to this day the fighter claims he never said anything. It's a moot point really because, *no mas* or not, his actions spoke louder than words. He had been humiliated by the antics of Leonard and was unable to catch him, and rather than suffer another seven rounds of embarrassment, and fatigue, he made the worst and most impulsive choice in his career.

Nobody could believe it, least of all Durán's trainer, Freddie Brown. 'He just quit. I've been with the guy nine years and I can't explain it. The guy is supposed to be an animal, you think an animal will fight right up until the end.'

For the fight Ray Leonard said, 'I did everything I said I was going to do, as he was too frustrated and confused. I did everything I could to make him go off, like a clock wound up too tight. He got wound up so tight he blew a spring.'

As the world turned against Durán, it was his home country of Panama where things were much worse; his kids were bullied at school, his mother's house was vandalized, rocks were hurled at his house. In his own defence he said: 'What was I supposed to do after beating Leonard in the first fight? Stay home, go to church every day and not screw around? That's just not me.'

Durán was far from finished. He picked himself back up and returned to the ring to fight David Moore in 1983 to win the WBA super welterweight championship. Marvin Hagler only beat him on a very narrow points decision to retain his WBC, WBA and IBF middleweight belts. Then later, at the vintage age of thirty-seven, Durán beat Iran Barkley and took his WBC middleweight crown, joining the elite club of those who have been champions in four different weight divisions.

Larry Holmes

Born in 1949, fatherless Holmes had to take care of himself aged thirteen and was a parent himself by the time he was seventeen. Competing as a professional boxer from 1973 to 2002, Holmes became world champion in 1978 and had one of the best ever left jabs in the sport. He was a good businessman outside of the ring and a very intelligent man despite a meagre education. Holding the WBC heavy-weight title from 1978 to 1983, as well as the IBF heavyweight title from 1983 to 1985, Holmes dodged no challengers and fought everyone, including Gerry Cooney, Mike Tyson, Muhammad Ali, Earnie Shavers, Tim Witherspoon, and many more. In fact he won the first forty-eight of his fights, falling only one short of Rocky Marciano's record forty-nine wins undefeated, when Holmes was beaten by Michael Spinks.

For four years, a young Larry Holmes had been a spar-ring partner of Ali's, and would put the knowledge of his training camps at Deer Lake to good use to later beat his master. For now, Holmes faced and felled the huge Roy Williams. He defeated the heavy punches of Earnie Shavers, which then won him a shot at the world title. After 'Neon' Leon Spinks had refused to face Ken Norton in pursuit of a more lucrative return bout with Ali, Norton was installed by the WBC as the heavyweight champ, and in 1978 Holmes was to be Norton's first defence of his title. What followed was to be one of the great fights in boxing history, with Holmes winning by a split decision, coming out on top by just a point.

In 1979 he went on to successfully defend his title sixteen times, an early fight facing Earnie Shavers, who dropped him in the seventh round with a blow that Holmes later spoke of as so powerful he thought his 'head had exploded'. Holmes got to his feet for the count, and stopped his opponent in the eleventh. In 1980 Holmes would reluctantly have to fight his mentor and idol, as Ali 'The Greatest' now came back out of retirement to stage an ill-advised comeback; the former champ was thirty-six and the years had taken their toll (Ali was said to be already suffering early onset Parkinson's disease). The fight went ten tragic rounds, with Ali barely throwing a punch. Out of respect for his old master, Holmes was not prepared to finish him off. Ali's corner finally called it a day.

Holmes went on to beat the likes of Trevor Berbick, Leon Spinks, Gerry Cooney, Marvis Frazier (son of Joe) and James 'Bonecrusher' Smith, putting him in grasping distance of beating Marciano's undefeated record of forty-nine victories. Holmes's forty-eighth fight was against the light heavyweight Michael Spinks, whom he loftily referred to as 'that skinny boy', who took the title from the long-reigning king.

Maybe he should've learnt a lesson in outstaying your longevity from Ali, but having beaten everybody and dodged *nobody* in his time, a thirty-eight-year-old Holmes in the 'beyond sunset' stage of his career, took on a young, newly crowned heavyweight champion, Mike Tyson, who at that time in his career was undefeated at thirty wins, with twenty-eight by knockout.

It was a slow start for Holmes who, thanks to his ring guile and longer reach, kept Tyson at bay, and in the third he showed some of his former flair as he danced around the ring, hurling that beautiful left jab with Swiss-watch precision. But like an army that never tires, Iron Mike kept up his assault and threw a left jab and killer right in the fourth. To his credit, Holmes was up for the count before an impatient Tyson was back at him, relentlessly knocking him down again before a vicious assault on a cornered Holmes; the upshot of which was another heavy right that poleaxed the old champ down on the canvas for the third time. Mercifully, the referee stopped the fight and declared a victory for Tyson by technical knockout.

Just because he gets old, it does not mean a fighter no longer considers himself a warrior; the fire burns inside him still, but his body is what lets him down. Larry Holmes staged one more comeback and won his next six fights, finally giving up his campaign after losing very respectably on points to Evander Holyfield.

Muhammad Ali

'I'm so fast that last night I turned off the light switch in my hotel room and was in bed before the room was dark.' Cassius Marcellus Clay Jr, born on 17 January 1942 in Louisville, Kentucky, for ever broke the boxing mould. In fact, Clay/Ali transcended the sport altogether. It wasn't just his good looks and statue-like frame, his rapier-quick wit, poetry and natural boxing ability that so enraptured the world for so long; Ali was a cultural phenomenon, and a spokesman of his time. His self-confidence was supreme, and so it should've been; he could dance across the canvas like Fred Astaire, his hand-speed a blur, they moved so fast. It wasn't just his fists that moved like lightning; out of his mouth flew a constant torrent of poetry, trash-talk, and in time, cultural truths which certain sections of white society didn't want to hear.

It's hard to imagine what the boxing landscape would've looked like without Ali. He clocked up one hundred fights as an amateur with five losses, and became the National Golden Globes champion aged seventeen. In 1961 he took the light heavyweight gold at the Rome Olympics. Cassius Clay was born into a restless time of social inequality and became a symbol of hope and a mouthpiece of resistance for Black America. He was also the new face of boxing and his arrival injected life back into a sport notorious for its corruption and connections with organized crime. Sonny Liston belonged to this old school, and when they met in Miami in 1964, Liston, the reigning heavyweight champion, was at a loss as to how he should handle the young, fast-talking Clay, whose talent was as prolific as his mouth. He couldn't catch him, he moved with such speed and grace. At round seven, Liston had had enough and refused to come out of his corner when the bell went. At age twenty-two, Clay was heavyweight champion of the world. By the time they had a rematch the following year, Cassius Clay had changed his name to Muhammad Ali and joined the Nation of Islam.

Headstrong and fearless, he was never one to keep quiet

about something he disagreed with, including when he refused to be drafted into the army for the Vietnam War. His punishment was to be stripped of his title and fined $10,000, and given a three-year ban, as well as being handed a five-year prison sentence. The story goes that the reason Ali began boxing was because somebody stole his bike when he was twelve and he was encouraged by a white police officer to take up boxing as a way to channel his anger. Overnight, he'd now become an enemy of the white state.

His battles with Joe Frazier are the stuff of legend, the first of which was in 1971 when – having beaten Joe Quarry and Oscar Bonavena – Ali attempted to win his title back after three long years in exile. The fight was magnificent, and it was Frazier who outpointed him and emerged victorious, but Ali – undeterred – went on to stun the world when he outboxed a seemingly invincible behemoth called George Foreman, who had taken Frazier's crown from him in 1973. Ali perfected the rope-a-dope method to beat him, by which much of the relentless banging he took from his opponent was transferred into the ropes. He went on to tire Foreman so badly he was able to knock him out in the eighth round.

He followed this with two defeats of Joe Frazier, the best being the Thrilla in Manila. Ali went on to fight some memorable bouts against boxers including Earnie Shavers and Ken Norton, losing his title to Leon Spinks, who he refought and beat seven months later. It's here he should have ended his dazzling days on a high, but boxing was to claim a high price from its most talented, prolific son, when Ali developed Parkinson's disease and was slowly enveloped by its cruel webbing, removing his most prized asset: his ability to communicate articulately. In 1999, he was voted Sportsman of the Century by *Sports Illustrated* and Sports Personality of the Century by the BBC. Personally, I will always remember Muhammad Ali as an individual as well as a champion of champions.

Mike Tyson

It has to be somebody pretty special that you name your son after, and Mike Gerald Tyson, born on 30 June 1966 in Brooklyn, New York, was just that. He was two when his father left the family to fend for themselves. Mike grew up with a lisp and was often in fights with boys who teased him for his impediment. Tyson and his family of three siblings were living on welfare, and his mother, struggling with a severe drink problem, was unable to enforce any authority on the young tearaway. Like so many future champions, his early, formative years could not have been any tougher, and by the time he was ten, young Tyson was well versed in the art of mugging and kicking the crap out of kids his age and older, as well as the odd adult, just for the hell of it.

Like my younger self, Mike was in and out of juvenile detention halls, and with over thirty arrests on his jacket, at the age of thirteen he looked set for a life in incarceration as his crimes became steadily more severe. But whilst doing a stint at the Tryon School for Boys, he was spotted by Bobby Stewart, who worked there, who taught him the basics of boxing in an attempt to teach him some discipline and to control his temper. Stewart was so impressed with the results from just a few lessons that he referred Tyson to seventy-two-year-old manager and trainer Cus D'Amato, an aged but brilliant teacher of the sweet science and the former coach of Floyd Patterson.

The wise old coach would become a kind of father-figure to this lisping wild boy of the streets, as he took Tyson under his wing, where he became part of the family, living and training in the peaceful Catskill Mountains outside of New York. Cus knew he had a future world champion on his hands. He wasn't just moulding the boy with boxing expertise, he was also imbuing him with the values that Mike had never learnt as a boy. After Mike's mum died when he was sixteen, Cus D'Amato became his legal guardian.

The young boxer possessed a natural strength and ability, and a burning hunger to win. In no time he was making a name for himself, having already won twenty-four of his twenty-seven amateur fights, as well as winning the National Golden Gloves heavyweight championship. Tyson turned professional in 1985, and that first year was nothing less than explosive, knocking out eleven of his fifteen opponents in the opening round. The following year he won another thirteen fights, including against Trevor

Berbick. Berbick went down in round four, losing his world heavyweight title and WBC belt, and Tyson became the youngest world heavyweight champion in history at just twenty years of age, beating Ali who as Cassius Clay had beaten Sonny Liston to claim the crown at just twenty-two.

It took Tyson ten months to unify all the belts, defeating James 'Bonecrusher' Smith for the WBA belt, and Tony Tucker for the IBF belt. Too fast and too fiery for the competition, he was almost literally ploughing through the best of the best with demonic hatred; anger seemed to radiate from his stocky frame. With his ducking, weaving and bobbing, he was reminiscent of Frazier; at the bell he flew out into the ring like a pit bull released from its chain. He seemed to take a dark pleasure in stripping other boxers down to nothing in as quick a time as possible. He destroyed Larry Holmes in four rounds, in revenge for what Holmes had done to his hero, Muhammad Ali, and knocked Michael Spinks out in the first round.

Cus D'Amato had died back in 1985 and, without his guiding wisdom, the cracks began to appear in the early 1990s when his stormy marriage to Robin Givens ended in divorce. He also broke with long-time manager Bill Cayton in favour of Don King, and sacked his trainer Kevin Rooney, who'd played such a big part in the champion's success. It was as if Tyson was smashing all the talismans that had insured protection from himself.

After nine successful defences, Tyson was beaten by James Buster Douglas in Tokyo, Japan, in 1990. In 1992 he was convicted of the rape of a beauty pageant contestant, serving three years of a six-year sentence for the crime.

After he came out of prison, he was never quite the same, despite winning the WBC belt from Frank Bruno, and the WBA belt from Bruce Seldon; the discipline that had once made him so dangerous seemed to have been replaced by a need to get the job done quickly, at any cost. By the time he was surgically taken apart by Lennox Lewis's jab and knocked out in the eighth round, he had become a shadow of himself.

I was so taken by the greatness of the young Tyson that I named my son after him. For all that his career ended sadly, nothing can take away the brilliance and savagery of those early professional years, when the world held its collective breath watching this aggressive and brilliant young boxer. Mike and I got to meet in 2023 in Saudi Arabia, when I was out there with Tommy for his fight against Jake Paul. We did a podcast together and I found him a very sensitive and emotional individual, as well as humble and self-deprecating. I like the person he has become and told him I'd like to share the ring with him. The door is still open to him.

Sugar Ray Leonard

Sugar Ray Leonard was born in Rocky Mount, North Carolina, in 1956, and named Ray Charles Leonard after the great musician. Unlike the boxers Mike Tyson and

Roberto Durán, his childhood was stable; he was an introverted kid who read comic books and played with his dog.
Like a lot of top athletes, he also struggled to fill the void
when he left his beloved sport. He is celebrated for the
dexterity and finesse he possessed in the ring; it was as if
he was able to slow time down, as the best athletes are,
making his opposition look clumsy and ponderous. There
are many who claim Sugar Ray Leonard was the most
skilful boxer ever to step in the ring.

He began his boxing career at the Parma Park recreation
centre. As an amateur he won 140 fights with five losses.
By the time he turned professional, he'd won two national
Golden Gloves Championships and a light welterweight
Olympic gold medal at the 1976 Olympics in Montreal.
In 1979 Leonard beat the reigning WBC welterweight
champion, Wilfred Benítez, but lost it within a year to the
infamous and legendary Roberto Durán. The wily
Panamanian had accosted Ray Leonard and insulted not
only him but also his wife in a park in Montreal, and the
tactic had worked; it was an unusually ruffled and angry
Sugar Ray who stepped into the ring that night. Durán
had gotten under his skin and Leonard attempted to fight
Durán toe-to-toe for the next fifteen rounds. Bad idea;
nobody liked rough-and-ready street-fighting as much as
Durán. It was a very different Ray Leonard at the rematch;
he wouldn't fall for that one again, and sure enough he
won back his title.

Leonard was a member of the Four Kings, a quartet of

the most distinguished and brilliant welterweight/middle-weights the world has ever seen at one time. The days of Benn, Eubank and Collins were terrific, but there was never a fourth king and, even had there been, let's say we added Calzaghe, they could never have measured up to the original four.

Not only did he have ring smarts, he was also a shrewd, calculating businessman with an eye for sponsorship deals. Much to the chagrin of Marvin Hagler, Ray skilfully nego-tiated paydays well above the amount of time he'd been a professional. His next opponent was Thomas Hearns, the reigning WBA welterweight champion. They met at Caesars Palace in what can only be described as a neck-and-neck brawl, which endured for fourteen gruelling rounds until the referee stopped the fight in favour of Leonard.

Sugar Ray was forced to retire twice because of a detached retina, before coming out of retirement to face Marvin Hagler for twelve rounds at Caesars Palace in 1987. Billed as The Super Fight, it was a bout that should have happened a few years earlier, when Hagler was still in his prime, though Ray Leonard was still the underdog at the bookies. Oddly, Hagler, a natural southpaw, began the fight in the orthodox stance and lost the first two rounds to Leonard. Leonard's speed and skills were in a different gear to Hagler, but the old champion continued to stalk him down and tire him out. Leonard won on a controver-sial split decision.

At the end of his career, Sugar Ray Leonard came out of retirement one last time to stop the unstoppable 'Macho Man' Héctor Camacho, after which he retired with a professional career record of thirty-six wins and three losses.

Old school greats

Jack Dempsey

One of nine children, Jack Dempsey was born in 1895 in Manassa, Colorado. He grew up poor, and had to fight for everything. As a teenager, he fought bare-knuckle for a few dollars in saloon bars and hobo camps. He started his professional boxing career in 1914, and quickly made a name for himself as a hard-hitting, aggressive fighter. Ferocity became his byword. His love of women and fine things ensured he became a symbol of the Roaring Twenties, and his trajectory from rags to riches was a good-luck story that inspired people in low stations to believe that anything could happen. But it would be a long hard journey to get there. Dempsey had all but given up on making a living from boxing when one of his brothers died, and to pay for the funeral he took a fight. Dempsey found management, and in his first year as a pro he fought a staggering twenty-one times.

Dempsey was a brawler, a rough-and-tumble fighter. He loved to fight his opponents toe-to-toe, where he could use his devastating left hook to great effect. It wasn't just power that made Dempsey a great fighter, he was also incredibly fast and agile, a master of footwork, always moving around the ring and looking for an opening to attack. He would dodge his opponents' punches and slip inside their defence.

His career really took off in the 1920s, when he became the heavyweight champion of the world. He had some incredible fights during this time, including his two famous battles with Gene Tunney. In their first fight, in 1926, Dempsey knocked Tunney down in the seventh round, but he couldn't finish him off. Tunney got up and went on to win the fight on points.

As far as I'm concerned, Dempsey was robbed in that fight. The ref gave Tunney a long count, and he should have been counted out. But Dempsey didn't complain; he was a true sportsman, and he respected his opponent. He came back in their rematch the following year, but lost again to Tunney in what would be his last fight. But it wasn't just his fights with Tunney that made Dempsey a legend. He had some incredible battles with other great fighters, like Luis Firpo and Jack Sharkey.

Dempsey, with his trademark black trunks and white shoes, was a real showman. He loved to entertain the crowd, and knew how to put on a good fight. It's often claimed that Dempsey brought boxing from the backwoods and into the American mainstream, and he was one of the first boxers who had the charisma and popularity to draw a million-dollar gate. Dempsey retired from boxing in 1928 with an incredible record: sixty-four wins, forty-nine by way of knockout, and six losses.

Jack Johnson

Born in Galveston, Texas, in 1878, Jack Johnson was to learn his craft as a boxer during a period of extreme racism, where the Black man had no rights and no access to the heavyweight crown. There were competitions called 'battle royal' where half-a-dozen Black men were put in the ring and the last man standing got to sweep up a few nickels and dimes that were thrown in by the white people at ringside. Maybe it was against five other men coming at him at the same time that Johnson developed his excellent defence. By 1903 he had beaten all the top contenders and was regarded as the best Black heavyweight in the world. But when it came to challenging James Jeffries, the reigning white heavyweight champion, the other refused to climb into the ring with a Black man.

Tommy Burns was the first heavyweight champ who finally agreed to box Johnson, though the latter had to chase him halfway round the world to Australia until Burns finally agreed to do so. They fought in Sydney in 1908, and Johnson taunted and outclassed him all the way through the fight until the fourteenth round. Johnson knocked Burns down in the first round and again in the seventh. It's said that Johnson could have knocked Burns out at any time; however, he seemed to be savouring taking it out on his opponent, as if Burns represented the white boxing establishment and all the abuse Johnson had suffered over the years.

The fight was stopped by the police in the fourteenth round and Jack Johnson became heavyweight champion of the world. It had been a hell of a hardship to get there, and Johnson was determined to enjoy his newfound fame and status, splashing earnings on flash motorcars, the finest of clothes, the best cigars and the most expensive champagne. White America resolved to get rid of him as soon as possible, and the best they could do to this end was bring James Jeffries out of retirement as the 'great white hope'. Johnson destroyed him, just as he had done Burns. The only way that they could get back at Johnson was by bending the law against him. Johnson's love of white women came back to haunt him, as he was prosecuted under the Mann Act, which prohibited the transportation of women across US state lines for immoral purposes, and he was sentenced to a year in prison. He fled to Europe before they could put him in jail. Allegedly, Johnson cut a deal with the American authorities to take a dive against the white six-foot-five-inch monster Jess Willard. They fought in Havana, Cuba, on 5 April 1915, and Jack Johnson was knocked out in the twenty-sixth round.

Rocky Marciano

Born Rocco Francis Marchegiano on 1 September 1923 in Brockton, Massachusetts (where Marvin Hagler would later live), Rocky Marciano took up boxing when he was drafted into the army in 1943, and won several competitions during the Second World War. As a sportsman he was an all-round athlete, who could turn his hand to baseball (he tried out for the Chicago Cubs) and American football.

Compared to the likes of Primo Carnera and Max Baer, Rocky Marciano was not a particularly arresting heavyweight proposition to look at; he was small and weighed just thirteen stone two pounds; his arms were short and he made for an easy target. But what made Marciano so special was his destructive punches and his resilience in the face of a hiding that would've left most boxers drawing their last breath.

By the time Rocky had knocked out his first sixteen opponents, promoters began to get wind of him. Having won his first thirty-seven fights, thirty-two of them by way of knockout, Marciano found himself climbing into the ring with his old hero, Joe Louis. Marciano knocked out an aged Louis in the eighth round, and it is said that he later cried in the old champion's dressing room, knowing that he had doused the light on a long and distinguished career.

In 1952 Marciano got a crack at the world heavyweight

title when he met the reigning champion, 'Jersey' Joe Walcott. Marciano went down in the first round and was outclassed and outboxed for the first thirteen rounds. Rocky landed a destructive right which put the other on the canvas beyond the count. On 27 April 1956, Marciano announced his retirement from boxing. He was only thirty-one and his unblemished record of forty-nine wins from forty-nine fights, with forty-three knockouts, is to this day still unbeaten.

'I was smart enough to buy
this land, now show me
that you're smart enough
to hang on to it.'

16

Keep What You Need, Not What You Want

Someone once asked me, 'Your son is one of the richest sportsmen on the planet, what are you doing stuck out in the middle of the countryside in an old 1950s caravan?' The best things in life are free, at least for me. I have acres and acres of farmland, and I can watch the sun rise unimpeded and I can watch it set. Now that's millionaire's paradise for me. I can cook my food on the fire and drink tea like generations of Travelling folk have done before me. Materialistic things don't interest me at all. People say: 'Your family are very wealthy.' Yes, perhaps, but not with me. I'm not a rich man, but I'm rich in other things. Besides, it's a cultural thing, Gypsies don't take off their kids, they give to them. I keep my life simple; that way there's less to worry about.

In the late eighties I had big ideas and was hungry to make as much money as I could. I wanted to impress others through my possessions. My father was different, though; as long as he had shelter, was clean and had food on the table, then that was enough for him. 'I've got a car, a vehicle to work with, a home to live in. I've got my strength and health, a good wife and I've got you and your brothers. What more could I possibly need?'

He used to say, 'I work to live, not live to work. What you need and what you want are two different things. Do you actually need more than you've got, son?' I couldn't answer him; he had me every time with that question.

'All these things you want,' he'd continue, 'are not what you need. They're accessories to make you look better in the eyes of people who really don't care whether you live or die.'

There are no morals today; it's all about the pound. And if people don't have much money, then they're not considered successful. Success should never be measured on how much money you've got in the bank, that's absurd. I'd much rather have a conversation with somebody who has plenty of substance to them and a story to tell, than a hollow billionaire with a fancy car but no morals and no interesting past. Broken people who've picked themselves back up again and tried to fix themselves are much more interesting than somebody who has never had any battles and has no scars on their hands or worry lines on their face.

In many ways the eighties were a bit like today, because everyone was in competition with each other over who had what. The whole 'keeping up with the Joneses' nonsense. In the decades before the eighties, people treated each other better; they remembered the hard times of the First World War, where so many young lives had been lost in the trenches; they remembered the rationing of the Second World War, the Nazi planes flying over dropping bombs on the cities, the wailing of sirens telling you to get underground.

The fifties were about rebuilding the country back up after the war, everyone doing their bit. Then came the sixties, with a healthy dose of counter-revolution in culture, and the seventies with the working class standing up against Thatcherism, which was shutting down mines and disbanding unions. Then the eighties arrived and created the 'yuppie', an odd-looking humanoid with padded shoulders and a brick-sized phone glued to its ear. Before then it wasn't about what you had, it wasn't about status, being working class was something you could be proud of.

In the days before the 'new money' wannabes of the eighties, you were either royalty or you weren't, and all the tea in China couldn't buy you blue blood. There was the upper class, the middle class and the working class, and people were proud about where they came from. Then, when the working classes started buying their council homes, it muddied the waters; working-class homeowners were now in a new aspirational lane called the 'lower middle-class', where all they had to do to fit in was to look the part, own things, splash the cash, wear the right clothes, drive the right car. It amused me to watch it happening. Yes, I had become a homeowner, but that wasn't because I wanted to rise up the social strata, I was just tired of moving around all my life and I wanted to establish roots. I didn't want be part of some new social set of so-called 'yuppies'.

I remember, during this period, I went on a Mediterranean cruise for two weeks. It was a big ship called *Oceania*, a luxury floating gin palace, stacked to the gills with restaurants serving every type of cuisine. *This is going to be good,* I'd thought to myself. I was seasick within the first hour. You could eat day and night, twenty-four hours per day; I must have put a stone and a half on in a fortnight . . . it was the best of food. But the other passengers on the ship, I just couldn't get on with them, because it was as if they were trying to pretend to be high society. Imagine it, there was a chef for every taste – Italian, French, British, Indian, Chinese – and all these wannabes were dressed up to the nines in their dinner jackets. I wandered down for some food on the first night wearing a pair of trainers, a T-shirt and some jogging pants and was told I was inappropriately dressed.

'Inappropriately dressed,' I said. 'We're not going to Buckingham Palace, are we?'

I had to go back to my room and put a suit on to eat. It felt like I was wearing a straitjacket. It all felt like a silly game.

To be honest, behind the rough exterior, I'm a bit of a

softy, and I'm a big one for nostalgia. Life is about making and gathering memories that you can hold dear in later life. Tyson once asked me if I wanted him to knock down my house so he could build a nicer one in its place, and I said, 'No, I couldn't. I've got so many memories of you and your brothers growing up here, of the family . . . my mum and dad, staying here, I couldn't knock it down.'

On another occasion, Tyson bought me a brand-new Rolls-Royce Phantom. First of all he claimed the car was for Paris, and asked me if I wouldn't mind driving it to the house for him. I said, 'What on earth does Paris need a car like this for? She's already got the RV and she can fit all the prams and the kids' stuff in that?' Tyson smiled, 'Actually, Dad, this is for you.'

I told him, 'You know, even if I was a rich man I wouldn't buy this car, because I don't need it. But the offer you just made is worth more to me than the car. I don't want your wealth, son. Just you keep winning, being a good dad and taking care of your health with your head screwed on, those are all the gifts that I want. And if ever I'm in need of a Roller, I need only ask you.'

The garage was in Knutsford, Cheshire, and I returned the keys to the man who'd sold Tyson the car and asked him to put the money back in my son's account.

'Well, that's the first time I've ever seen one of these returned!' he said.

'What my son's achieved in the ring and the man that he is today are more than enough for me.'

There's a big difference between needing and wanting, and if I don't *need* something it has no place in my home. It wasn't the fact that the Roller cost around half a million pounds, that wasn't the issue, the issue was, I didn't need it. I keep very little in my life that doesn't have a purpose or use. I'm not materialistic, my house isn't extravagant. It is cosy, with a lovely old grate where a fire is perpetually burning, and a fine view of my field, but it's not in any danger of appearing in *Country Living* magazine any time soon. My one weakness is old inexpensive cars from the 1980s, and I underline the word 'inexpensive'. I'm a bit of a collector of strays in need of a home because I have such a fondness for the past. When you rescue an old rusty motor, it's like having a fragile bird in your hand and helping it fly again, and in my back yard you'll find anything from an antique Land Cruiser and Land Rover to an Austin Herald. The things I'm most proud of, though, are my wooden, hand-carved Romani wagons, as they connect me directly to my people and roots.

When I was growing up, food and heating were not a given, and clothes were scarce. Everything was hard work, like showering outside in the winter. Not to sound like that Monty Python sketch about poverty and living in a hole in the road, but sometimes when we showered outside, it could be three or four below zero. If we were parked up somewhere which was two miles from the nearest garage with a water tap, then I would have to walk with two empty five-gallon cans, fill them up and walk back again, stopping every hundred yards to catch my breath. I hated having to strip down to my underpants to give myself a good scrub in that freezing weather, and part of me dreamed about having a house where I could have a shower without catching my death of cold. My dad kindly created a tent at the back of the trailer where we could shower in privacy, but it didn't keep the chill away. I wanted a better life for my children, an easier start for them than I had had. I'd like to think I've achieved that. My life is my family; without my boys I wouldn't have a purpose in life. At best I would have been a sad and lonely man with a bad temper, a loose cannon going through life as best as he could.

Though I tend to keep my own company and am a bit of a loner, I'm not self-absorbed, or overly interested in myself. Nowadays people are so scared and obsessed about what other people think about them. It's not healthy when people make grand assumptions about someone else's life based on a photo; where you're made to feel as if you're failing because you don't drive as nice a car as a school friend, who you've not seen for thirty years but happen to spot on Instagram. It's not a charitable world we live in; rather than being happy for any success you might have, people tend to feel threatened. Or they're happy for you so long as you're not doing as well as them, or god forbid that you are doing better! Then they become resentful. I have an old Rolls-Royce sat in the shed and I never drive it. I prefer to get about in an old 1980s VW Golf because that way I attract less attention and green eyes. I don't do

Facebook, or have a Twitter or Instagram account.

The older you get, the more you should try and simplify your life, keeping stress at bay and focusing on making the most of the time you have left. I've always preferred to be rich in experience rather than rich with money in the bank. The land my house sits on, plus the surrounding fields, is probably worth far in excess of £4 million. About thirty years ago, when I was living a dangerous life and there was a good chance I was bound for an early grave, I signed it over to my sons, and said to them: 'I was smart enough to buy this land, now show me that you're smart enough to hang on to it.' I like to think that they will never sell it to a property developer, but instead preserve this little patch of green where they had such fun growing up and made so many happy memories.

What I can say is that what you

see is what you get, and

you will never be in doubt of

where you are with me.

Epilogue

My mother used to say, 'Let your "yes" be your yes and let your "no" be your no. Put your best foot forward and be as strong as you can.' In other words: be yourself and be true to your word. I've certainly followed this advice but it hasn't always landed well with others; I'm often regarded as being outspoken and tricky to deal with. What I can say is that what you see is what you get, and you will never be in doubt of where you are with me.

I've always looked for genuine people at every turn. People speak rubbish to make conversation and there is an awful lot said of me that is just not true. I am an awkward fellow, I know that, but I wear my heart on my sleeve and listen to my intuition when it comes to people.

Some days I think I am the most misunderstood person on earth. That's one of the reasons that I've written this book. At first I worried that people might think I was riding on the coat-tails of my son Tyson, that I was skimming the bubbles of his fame. That couldn't be further from the truth. All I want is to tell you my story, to share with you the dark and the light of my own journey, and describe some of the adventures this Gypsy has been lucky enough to have experienced.

When you grow up like I did with nothing, and I mean nothing, you want to do as much as you can to ensure things are easier for your kids than they were for you. At seventeen years old I was a young father, and I regarded it as the greatest of responsibilities. I had no education, no help, but I wanted to teach my kids to be tough enough to handle most situations. I have been very lucky, and there must be somebody up there who likes me because despite the life I've led – the trials and tribulations, sadness, tears, dying, the suffering and the pain – I'm still here and on top today at fifty-eight years old. I've had six sons, I've looked after two families. All my sons have surpassed me in their successes and are better than me in every way. They have clean characters and that means a lot to me. I could pass away tonight and be satisfied with what I've managed to achieve with them. For all that we have our squabbles, we have an unbreakable bond and would die for each other.

When I was in prison Tyson asked me, 'Is there any

place on your bucket list you'd like to go to once you get out of here, Dad?'

'Pompeii,' I said.

'Right then, we're going,' he said.

We didn't manage to get out there for one reason or another until earlier this year. But it was worth the wait, just to spend quality time with Tyson and to see him so happy. Along with two friends, neither of them small men, we hired a Fiat Punto and drove to Pompeii to see the village where the lava had burnt the ancient city's population to death, during the great eruption of Mount Vesuvius in 79 CE. It was a bit of a squeeze in that car! The Amalfi Coast was beautiful, and on our last day we drove to Capri and then had a skinful of Italian beer. Sat out in the sunshine, it was absolutely glorious, I'll never forget it, it was one of those 'pinch yourself' moments when you look at your life and you feel pure gratitude. This radiant happiness was rudely punctured by the realization that we were flying that afternoon and needed to get back to the airport! The problem, however, was we were all well beyond tipsy . . . One of us had to drive back along the Amalfi Coast, which you may or may not know is one of the most dangerous roads in the world, hugging the cliffs above the Tyrrhenian Sea, infamous for its narrowness, hairpin bends, sheer drops, and staggering views of the abyss just outside your car door. Thankfully I managed to sober up before it was time to drive and we made the flight in the nick of time.

Life is about these special moments and adventures. What is past is past, it can't be changed. Look to the sun and to the future, savour the present and, till next time we meet, God bless you and keep you safe.

Acknowledgements

I would like to thank my co-writer Richard Waters for his hard work and skill in telling my story and for the fact we are now friends. My gratitude too to the Editorial team at Pan Macmillan and all who have worked on the book on my behalf. My final thanks go to my sons and family who have agreed to appear in these pages.

Picture acknowledgements

Plate section one

All images courtesy of the author.

Plate section two

1. Tyson and John, 2006 © David Oates Photography/Alamy.
2. Tyson celebrates John McDermott win © TGSPHOTO /Alamy.
3. Training with Tyson for Klitschko © Julian Finney/Getty.
4. Tyson vs Klitschko © Associated Press/Alamy.
5. Tyson celebrates winning world heavyweight title in 2015 © AP Photo/Martin Meissner.
6. John at homecoming event in Bolton © Simon Cooper/Alamy.
7. Tyson celebrating Wilder win © Ethan Miller/Getty.
8. John and Tommy training in Box Park © Justin Setterfield/ Getty.
9. Second image of John and Tommy training in Box Park © Nick Potts/Alamy.
10. Roman Fury vs Erik Nazaryan © Simon Marper/Alamy.
11. Celebrating Tommy's win against Jake Paul in Riyadh © Francois Nel/Getty.
12. Training with the boys in Manchester. Image courtesy of Roman Fury.
13. John and Roman in the Peak District. Image courtesy of Roman Fury.
14. Outside the Winchester caravan with John's mother. Image courtesy of the author.
15. John with vintage car. Image courtesy of the author.

JOHN'S FIGHTING FAMILY TREE
(On father's side)

Bartley Gorman
(Born 1836, fought end of the nineteenth century)
Great-great-grandfather

Ticker Gorman
(Born 1906, fought 1920–1940)
Great-uncle

Bartley Gorman
(Born 1944, fought 1972–1992)
One of the best Gypsy Kings ever
Third cousin

'Big John' Fury
(Born 1965, fought 1987–1995)
Professional boxer
Unbeaten bare-knuckle fighter

Tyson 'The Gypsy King' Fury
(Born 1988, fighting since 2007)
Current WBC world heavyweight champion
Lineal world heavyweight champion

Tommy Fury
(Born 1999, fighting since 2018)
Professional cruiserweight boxer

JOHN'S FIGHTING FAMILY TREE

(On mother's side)

George 'Digger' Stanley
(Born 1876, fought 1908–1911)
World bantamweight champion
Great-great-great-cousin

Ned, Tom and Crope Skeet
(Fought 1930s)
Bare-knuckle fighters
Great-uncles

John Fury was born on 22 May 1965. He is a retired professional boxer and bare-knuckle fighter of Irish and British descent.